DEDICATION

I dedicate this dissertation to my family, friends, and colleagues.

ABSTRACT

Merger and Acquisition Integration: Exploring Uncertainty from the Perspective of the Middle Manager

Purpose. The purpose of this qualitative study was to explore middle managers' perceptions about how organizations managed job-related, structural, and strategic uncertainty during a merger and acquisition (M&A) integration process. Furthermore, this research investigated what strategies middle managers perceived effective and ineffective for managing uncertainty and recommendations for managing uncertainty during future integrations.

Methodology. This qualitative study utilized a phenomenological research design that collected data through open-ended interviews. Fifteen middle managers participated in the study and were asked 12 questions that explored their perceptions about managing uncertainty during an M&A integration.

Findings. Overall, participants perceived strategic uncertainty was managed well, structural uncertainty was managed poorly, and job-related uncertainty was mixed. Effective strategies for managing job-related uncertainty focused on communication, whereas effective strategies for managing strategic and structural uncertainty included clear visions, defined roles and responsibilities, and opportunities to collaborate. Recommendations for managing all types of uncertainty were related to communicating, planning, interacting as a team, and valuing employees.

Conclusions. Most organizations are not managing M&A processes well. Companies need to adequately manage information from the onset of the M&A until full integration is achieved to avoid adverse effects and reduce uncertainty. Communication through in-person roadshows, websites, and newsletters helped employees gain a better understanding of why the change was occurring, which reduced uncertainty. Organizations could better use middle managers during M&A processes to create structure, build trust, disseminate information, and reduce uncertainty, which could lead to a more successful integration process.

Recommendations. The success of an M&A often pivots on the integration process. Additional academic and applied research is needed to build on the body of knowledge about M&As, with specific emphasis given to the integration process. During an M&A, executives need to establish the direction for the integration process and prioritize intentional communication. A dedicated integration team should be appointed to develop a comprehensive integration plan, implement the plan, and monitor the integration process to ensure appropriate course corrections. Middle managers should be given additional training to best support the M&A integration process.

TABLE OF CONTENTS

CHAPTER I: INTRODUCTION
   Background
      <u>Merger and Acquisition Integration Process</u>
      Uncertainty
      Middle Managers
      Ways to Reduce Uncertainty
   Statement of the Research Problem
   Purpose Statement
   Research Questions
   Significance of the Problem
   Definitions
   Delimitations
   Organization of the Study

CHAPTER II: LITERATURE REVIEW
   Mergers and Acquisitions
      Competition
      Synergy
      Growth
      Merger and Acquisition Success and Value
      Merger and Acquisition Failure
   Merger and Acquisition Integration Processes
      Complexity
   Change
   Uncertainty
      Types of Uncertainty
      Impacts of Uncertainty on the Employee
   Middle Managers
   Employee Reaction to Uncertainty
      Stress and Anxiety
      Resistance
      Conflict
      Job Uncertainty and Turnover
   Ways to Reduce Uncertainty
      Organizational Communication
      Trust
      Fairness
      Engagement

      Commitment
      Planning
      Decision-Making
      Vision
      Culture
      Routines and Norms
      Group Identification
   Summary

CHAPTER III: METHODOLOGY
   Purpose Statement
   Research Questions
   Research Design
   Population
   Sample
      Selection Criteria
   Instrumentation
      Instrument Validity and Reliability
   Data Collection
   Data Analysis
   Limitations
   Summary

CHAPTER IV: RESEARCH, DATA COLLECTION, AND FINDINGS
   Purpose Statement
   Research Questions
   Research Methods and Data Collection Procedures
   Population
   Sample
   Demographic Data
   Presentation and Analysis of Data
   Findings for Research Question One
      Perceptions of Managing Job-Related Uncertainty
      Perceptions of Managing Structural Uncertainty
      Perceptions of Managing Strategic Uncertainty
   Findings for Research Question Two
      Effective Strategies for Managing Job-Related Uncertainty
      Effective Strategies for Managing Structural and Strategic Uncertainty
   Findings Related to Research Question Three
      <u>Ineffective Strategies for Managing Uncertainty</u>
   Findings Related to Research Question Four

Recommendations Across all Types of Uncertainty
Recommendations for Managing Job-Related Uncertainty
Recommendations for Managing Structural Uncertainty
Recommendations for Managing Strategic Uncertainty
Summary

CHAPTER V: FINDINGS, CONCLUSIONS, & RECOMMENDATIONS
Review of the Problem
Purpose Statement
Research Questions
Research Methods and Data Collection Procedures
Major Findings
    Research Question One
    Research Question Two
    Research Question Three
    Research Question Four
Unexpected Findings
Conclusions
Implications for Action
Recommendations for Future Research
Concluding Remarks and Reflections

REFERENCES

APPENDICES

LIST OF TABLES

Table 1. Uncertainty Synthesis Matrix

Table 2. Dates for Participant Communication and Interviews.

Table 3. Industry Breakdown of Study Participants

Table 4. Number of Themes by Research Question and Type of Uncertainty

Table 5. Perceptions of How the Companies Managed Uncertainty by Type

Table 6. Effective Strategies for Managing Uncertainty During Integration

Table 7. Ineffective Strategies for Managing Uncertainty During Integration

Table 8. Recommendations for Managing Uncertainty

CHAPTER I: INTRODUCTION

Mergers and acquisitions (M&As) are strategies regularly utilized in the global business community to increase value, profitability, and growth as businesses strive to gain a competitive advantage in their respective industries. Within the last few years, the international community steadily increased the use of M&As with North American companies projected to keep leading this trend (Deloitte Development [Deloitte], 2015, 2016; KPMG, 2014). Annually, trillions of dollars are invested in this activity; however, M&As are plagued with high rates of failure (Kim & Roumeliotis, 2014; Shermon, 2011). Although the research varied greatly, it indicated over 65% of M&As ultimately failed to meet expectations and 53% of these deals decreased the value of the organizations (Doseck, 2012; Harding & Rouse, 2007; Marks & Mirvis, 2011). Consequently, companies must confront the difficult decision whether to invest in an M&A given the high risks.

Research indicated the value created from an M&A was highly dependent upon the integration process (Doseck, 2012;

Marks & Mirvis, 2011). Integration is the process that occurs after an M&A focused on bringing together the two previously separate companies to create a new organization (Knilans, 2009). Integration processes tend to be extremely complex and when managed poorly value can be lost, negating potential profits of the M&A's original goals (Dickinson, 2013; Schwieger & Very, 2003; Vasilaki, 2011; Weber, Tarba, & Oberg, 2014). Some argue M&A integrations are essentially major organizational changes, which inherently make them both complex and challenging to effectively execute (Clayton, 2010; Hahm, Jung, & Moon, 2013; Jacobs, van Witteloostujin, & Christe-Zeyse, 2013; Sun, 2011). Kansal and Chandani (2014) suggested the integration process resulted in complex changes to legal, information technology and accounting systems, the organizational structure, goals and strategies, human resource processes, the financial market, and government regulations. As organizations undergo complex change, uncertainty naturally rose as human dynamics increased (Burke, 2013; Mahajan, 2011; Shook, Priem, & McGee, 2003).

When employees feel their livelihoods are threatened by the uncertainty of the future, they tend to resort to actions to reduce or avoid it (Khan, 2013). Counterproductive behaviors can seriously impact an organization, unless middle managers effectively respond to employee reactions to the change (Allan & Cianni, 2011; Gilley, McMillan, & Gilley, 2009). More specifically, middle managers can influence integration success because they are generally in tune with employee needs and have access to both frontline employees and executives (Gerds, Strottmann, & Jayaprakash, 2010; Sanders & Frenkel, 2011). Middle managers also direct frontline employees responsible for implementing the organization's plans (Dean & Cianni, 2011). When uncertainty runs rampant within an organization, middle managers must work to mitigate the negative effects by implementing intervention processes, including building trust and communication, anchoring to a compelling vision, and establishing a nurturing culture (Anderson-Ackerman & Anderson 2010; Armstrong, 2011; Baldwin, 2012; DePamphilis, 2014; Funk, 2011). Despite the role of executing these interventions during an integration process, middle managers are often overlooked and underutilized through the M&A process (Anderson, 2012).

Background

The use of M&As grew globally over the last few decades (Daly, Pouder, & Kabanoff, 2004; Shermon, 2011; Institute for Mergers, Acquisitions & Alliances [IMAA], 2018a). One driving factor was the sentiment the combination of two companies will be a greater entity than if the two organizations remained separate (King, Dalton, Daily, & Covin, 2004; Marks & Mirvis, 2011). Other driving factors included a desire to remain competitive in the business environment and the need to pursue inorganic organizational growth (George, 2011; Maepa, 2014). A primary goal of M&As is to increase the profitability and value for the combined organization (Doseck, 2012; Zollo & Singh, 2004). Although businesses utilize M&As as a viable advancement and expansion strategy, these transactions carry considerable risk, as evidenced by the failure rates associated with M&A activity (De Hoyos, 2013; Marks & Mirvis, 2011; Tikhomirov & Spangler, 2009; Vazirani & Mohaptra, 2012).

With failure rates reported to range from 40% to 80%, the risks associated with M&As are weighty (Bertoncelj & Kovac, 2007; Dunbar, 2013; Valant, 2009; Waldman & Javidan, 2009). Harding and Rouse (2007) found 53% of companies experience a decline in organizational value following an M&A. Despite these risks, which are widely documented in the literature and media, M&As continue to increase with over a trillion dollars spent on M&A activity each year (Deloitte, 2015; Kim & Roumeliotis, 2014; KPMG, 2014; Weber & Drori, 2011). Within the United States, over $1.7 trillion was invested in M&As in 2017 alone (IMAA, 2018a). This suggests considerable capital and resources are wasted because of a limited understanding behind the successes and failures of M&A activity. Many experts believe failures occur because of poorly managed integration processes (Doseck, 2012; Dunbar, 2013).

Uncertainty

The integration process combines two individual companies into a single organization (Knilans, 2009). Some experts suggested the process had considerable bearing on whether a venture will achieve the goals outlined at the onset of the M&A (Doseck 2012; Marks & Mirvis, 2011). Although largely accepted, the literature provided no unified or standardized approach to planning, conducting, and assessing integration processes (Schmidt, 2008; Weber & Drori, 2011). Weber et al. (2014) described the integration process as interactive and gradual with workforces from both businesses coming together to share abilities and resources. Given the complexities of this type of change effort, integration processes demand "skill, diligence, and patience" within the newly formed organization

(Braun, 2013, p. 207). Not surprising, the research revealed companies undergoing integration processes encountered more disruption than counterparts not undergoing an M&A (Puranam, Singh, & Zollo, 2006). In addition to disrupting the productivity of the newly joined company, failed integration efforts waste valuable resources, such as time and money, and have the potential to negatively impact employee performance and satisfaction (Money, 2011; Shermon, 2011; Wallis, Steptoe, & Cole, 2006). To reduce this potential loss of resources, middle managers must carefully navigate the challenges that inevitably come from increased uncertainty during times of wide scale change.

Merger and Acquisition Integration Process

The literature characterized uncertainty as a "lack of knowledge about current or future events" (Bordia, Hobman, Jones, Gallois, & Callan, 2004, p. 512). By their nature, integration processes often resulted in high levels of uncertainty, leading employees to need more information to fill the void and therefore function effectively in their day-to-day roles (Anderson-Ackerman & Anderson 2010; Armstrong, 2011). Without this additional information, uncertainty generated resistance from employees and created conflicts (Anderson-Ackerman & Anderson, 2010; Bercovitz & Feldman, 2008; Danişman, 2010; Weber, Tarba, & Reichel, 2011).

Uncertainty presented itself in different forms, such as job-related, structural, and strategic uncertainty (Bordia et al., 2004). Job-related uncertainty focused on how uncertainty affected employees at an individual level. Structural uncertainty focused on day-to-day operations and outcomes when faced with uncertainty. Strategic uncertainty focused on the influence of uncertainty on the whole organization and its future (Bordia et al., 2004). When faced with heightened job-related, structural, and strategic uncertainties during an integration process, employees reacted with any number of behaviors, including stress, anxiety, job insecurity, and turnover (Baldwin, 2012; Clayton 2010; De Dreu & Gelfand, 2008; Erwin & Garman, 2010; Geiselmann, 2012; Vander Elst, Baillien, De Cuyper, & De Witte, 2010). Allan and Cianni (2011) suggested organizations utilize middle managers to stop uncertainty from running rampant and generating resistance, conflict, and other negative reactions.

Middle Managers

During an integration process, middle managers were considered key influencers as they had the greatest access to help employees through this major change initiative (Allan & Cianni, 2011). In this capacity, these managers serve as an important conduit for connecting priorities from senior management and relaying those directives to frontline employees (Osterman, 2008; Stoker, 2006). Osterman (2008) contended "managers make organizations run" and middle managers were influential in the outcomes of many business activities. In this context, middle managers were the linchpins between organizational goals and daily activities, creating a unique opportunity to manage uncertainty and influence the integration process (Allan & Cianni, 2011). Despite this potential, middle managers often faced challenges associated with limited assistance and resources, which hindered their abilities to effectively navigate an integration process (Anderson, 2012).

Ways to Reduce Uncertainty

To effectively manage a change process of this magnitude, the research suggested that managers understood the factors at play to reduce uncertainty (Armstrong, 2011). Specific ways to reduce uncertainty included increasing communication, establishing trust, setting out a clear vision, and protecting and building shared culture. The research suggested the use of effective communication helped to reduce uncertainty during the organizational transition because the more information an employee had about his or her situation, the easier it was for him or her to handle the number of organization changes that occurred during integration processes (Bordia et al. 2004; Vazirani & Mohapatra, 2012). The research inferred trust should be focused on the manager and employee interactions and how that impacted the perceived fairness of the decisions, workforce engagement, and employee commitment (Armstrong, 2011; Fedor, Caldwell, & Herold, 2006; Maepa, 2014; Mann, 2011). Activities tied to operating and directing the company such as strategic planning, transparent decision-making, and setting a clear and compelling vision were also thought to help reduce uncertainty because they increased employee buy-in (Armstrong, 2011; Funk, 2011; Jarrard, 2014). By their nature, integration processes disrupted the organization's culture, causing questions about shared values and norms that caused additional uncertainty. Best practices suggested efforts to protect culture could reduce uncertainty (Allatta & Singh, 2011; Appelbaum, Roberts, & Shapiro, 2009; Mahajan, 2011). Although these dynamics impact uncertainty, no detailed information exists on which interventions are perceived as most effective during an M&A integration process, creating a need for further exploration.

Statement of the Research Problem

M&As increased in frequency over the last few decades as globalization forced businesses to seek alternative means of growth (Daly et al., 2004). This surge was accompanied by over $1.7 trillion funneled into M&A business activity in the United States during 2017 (Kim & Roumeliotis, 2014; KPMG, 2014; IMAA, 2018a). Deloitte (2015) analyzed M&A trends in their 2015 quarterly report, which indicated M&A activity in 2015 increased by nearly 25% over 2014 numbers. The amount of capital invested into M&As suggested these transactions have become increasingly important in the business community; however, despite these increases, research also showed M&As failed at alarming rates (Dunbar, 2013; Waldman & Javidan, 2009).

Although the research on failure rates varied, estimates indicated over 65% of M&As failed to achieve their goals, which resulted in financial and productivity losses (DePamphilis, 2009; Doseck, 2012; Marks & Mirvis, 2011). Harding and Rouse (2007) further suggested 53% of firms experienced a decrease in overall company value as the result of an M&A. The greatest probability for failure of M&As occurred during the integration process (Appelbaum, Lefrancois, Tonna, & Shapiro, 2007; Weber & Drori, 2011). This was especially problematic as established M&A goals often relied heavily upon the integration process, as the organizations aimed to consolidate operations to reduce redundancy, capitalize on synergies, expand market share, and ultimately increase value (Venema, 2015). Despite the importance of the integration process, integration processes were often inadequately executed, demonstrating disconnects between those driving the overall business strategy and execution on the part of the middle managers and frontline employees (Björkman, Stahl, & Vaara, 2007; Lakshman, 2011; Zollo & Singh, 2004).

The research was clear that high levels of uncertainty negatively impacted organizational effectiveness and productivity (PricewaterhouseCoopers [PwC], 2011). Thus, integration processes will continue to be undermined by employees until a better understanding of uncertainty emerges (Guindon, 2013; Mann, 2011). Both Waldman and Javidan (2009) and Weber and Drori (2011) suggested more comprehensive data are needed to clearly understand how to more effectively manage an M&A integration process. Simply stated, with over 65% of companies failing to properly integrate and realize preset expectations, new understandings need to pave the way for more sound and predictable business activity (Doseck, 2012; Marks & Mirvis, 2011).

Purpose Statement

The purpose of this qualitative study was to explore middle managers' perceptions about how organizations managed job-related, structural, and strategic uncertainty during a merger and acquisition (M&A) integration process. Furthermore, this research investigated what strategies middle managers perceived effective and ineffective for managing job-related, structural, and strategic uncertainty during an M&A integration process. Finally, this study worked to identify the strategies middle managers recommended to manage job-related, structural, and strategic uncertainty during an M&A integration process.

Research Questions

The following research questions guided this study:

1. How did middle managers perceive organizations managed job-related, structural, and strategic uncertainty during an M&A integration process?
2. What strategies did middle managers perceive to be effective for managing job-related, structural, and strategic uncertainty during an M&A integration process?
3. What strategies did middle managers perceive to be effective for managing job-related, structural, and strategic uncertainty during an M&A integration process?
4. What recommendations did middle managers make for managing job-related, structural, and strategic uncertainty during an M&A integration process?

Significance of the Problem

M&As continue to be an often-used strategy to increase value for companies within the global business community as evidenced by the significant amount of money spent on these transactions every year (Weber et al., 2014). With M&A average failure rates estimated at 65%, companies face serious risks for expending organizational resources that may never realize projected goals (DePamphilis, 2009; Doseck, 2012; Marks & Mirvis,

2011). Inability to successfully integrate organizations during an M&A can have a devastating impact on a company's value and profitability (Weber et al., 2011). Furthermore, organizations that failed to integrate properly had the potential to lose their competitive advantage in the global market by consuming resources without reaping the benefits of the M&A (Baldwin, 2012). Future M&A transactions are in jeopardy of the same failure that plagued the current business landscape unless a greater understanding around the integration process can be achieved.

The research suggested failures that occurred during M&A integration processes linked back to challenges stemming from uncertainty. Managers could handle their jobs within the organization but were not trained or effectively prepared to manage integration processes (Allan & Cianni, 2011; Appelo, 2010). Training managers also required greater insights and a more thorough understanding of how to effectively manage uncertainty during an M&A integration process (Peloquin, 2011).

This study explored middle managers' perceptions regarding how organizations managed job-related, structural, and strategic uncertainty during an M&A integration process. The study further explored the strategies middle managers perceived as effective or ineffective to manage job-related, structural, and strategic uncertainty during an M&A integration process. Additionally, the study worked to identify strategies middle managers recommended to manage job-related, structural, and strategic uncertainty during an M&A integration process. The knowledge generated from this study could provide companies with relevant information regarding how to effectively manage job-related, structural, and strategic uncertainty during an M&A integration process.

Definitions

Change. Change is a natural and complex process of developing and evolving an organization from the interactions that occur between various organizational members (Jian, 2011; Thomas, Sargent, & Hardy, 2011).

Integration. Integration is "a fundamental stage within a merger and acquisition that actually brings together the organizations that were previously separated" (Doseck, 2012, p. 23).

Job-Related Uncertainty. A form of uncertainty focused on employees at an individual level (Bordia et al., 2004).

Mergers & Acquisitions (M&As). Mergers are "a combination of two companies to form a new company" and acquisitions are "the purchase of one company by another in which no new company is formed" (Whitaker, 2012, p. 7).

Middle Manager. Middle managers direct day- to-day activities and operations with subordinate employees based on the direction provided by top management personnel (Ferry, 2010).

Strategic Uncertainty. A form of uncertainty focused on the rationale for the change, the organization's direction, and the shifting environment of the organization (Bordia et al., 2004).

Structural Uncertainty. A form of uncertainty focused on the day-to-day operations of systems and structures in an organization (Bordia et al., 2004).

Uncertainty. Uncertainty refers to employees getting a shortage of necessary information about their given circumstances or situations (Schweiger & Very, 2003).

Uncertainty Reduction. Uncertainty reduction refers to any actions taken by an individual, group of employees, or organization to reduce uncertainty about organizational events (Jarrard, 2014; Khan, 2013; Venema, 2015).

Delimitations

The population was limited to middle managers who worked in organizations with operations in the southern California region of the United States. Another delimitation included the selection criteria for middle managers, which required them to be involved in an M&A integration process within the last three years and managed subordinates during that time.

Organization of the Study

In Chapter I, the topic of the research was introduced in addition to the problem, purpose, research questions, significance, definitions, and delimitations. Chapter II delves deeper into the literature and provides a background on M&A activity, integrations, uncertainty, middle managers, and organizational interventions for uncertainty. The methodology for data collection and analysis for this research study are examined in Chapter III. Chapter IV presents a detailed account of the research findings with an analysis of the results related to the research questions. Finally, Chapter V explores the study findings and conclusions, as well as implications and recommendations for future research.

CHAPTER II: LITERATURE REVIEW

Chapter II includes a review of the literature that explored the background and reasoning for this study. This chapter was separated into the following sections: mergers and acquisitions, integration processes, change, uncertainty, middle managers, employee reactions to uncertainty, ways to reduce uncertainty, and a summary.

Mergers and Acquisitions

Mergers and acquisitions (M&As) continued to be used as a strategy for business growth and the number of deals grew over time (Weber & Drori, 2011). An M&A occurs when two or more organizations join together to form a single company that may share a name as well as resources and goals (Baldwin, 2012; Marks & Mirvis, 2011). The literature suggested mergers slightly differ from acquisitions, with mergers often being a combination and acquisitions generally defined as one organization taking control of another (Cummings & Worley, 2008;

Funk, 2011; Steele, 2014). International M&A data suggested that as of 2017, there were 51,919 M&A transactions totaling 3.6 trillion dollars (IMAA, 2018a). International trends for 2016 revealed most M&A deals were conducted in the United States with significant activity occurring in North America (Deloitte, 2016). M&As continued to increase in usage by businesses around the world with over $3.7 trillion of activity occurring internationally in 2017 (IMAA, 2018a). Lodorfos & Boateng, 2006; Weber & Drori, 2011).

Many companies operate in a global business environment and experience high rates of change and complexity (George, 2011). Maepa (2014) confirmed organizations must function in a "dynamic evolving environment where change is a constant reality" (p. 1). Within this business environment, M&As became the preeminent activity for expansion over the last three decades, with transactions generally focused on bolstering company performance (Tikhomirov & Spangler, 2009; Vazirani & Mohapatra, 2012). The literature suggested M&As are pursued by organizations for different reasons, with the three most common reasons being: (1) to stay competitive, (2) to achieve synergy, and (3) to see inorganic growth (Armstrong, 2011; Dickinson, 2013; Dunbar, 2013; Funk, 2011; George, 2011; Peloquin, 2011; Reider, 2011).

Competition

Companies pursued M&As for competitive purposes, sometimes embarking on this massive undertaking "out of competitive necessity for survival" (George, 2011, p. 46). Ferry (2010), George (2011), Maepa (2014), and Quinonez-Gonzalez (2013) agreed companies need strategies to survive and stay competitive, especially within a highly turbulent business atmosphere. Reider (2011) argued M&As could make companies more competitive because they enabled an organization to immediately respond when "competition offers new product features, better pricing, or alternate solutions" (p. 14). Baldwin (2012) and Bellou (2006) further suggested M&As allowed companies to compete at a global level and establish competitive positions they would not achieve through other organizational advancement strategies.

Synergy

Synergy was another strategic rationale for M&As because the combination of two companies purportedly produced more value than an individual entity (Dickinson, 2013; Marks & Mirvis, 2011). A company that pursued M&As with the rationale of synergy looked to increase organizational value by leveraging complementary resources (KPMG, 2011). The reasoning behind this approach was two organizations coming together captured a larger share of the market and allowed more to be accomplished as an integrated entity than as individual organizations (DePamphilis, 2009; Doseck, 2012; Kale & Singh, 2009). Dunbar (2013) acknowledged M&As should look to "leverage synergies, market share, intellectual property, and talent within the organization" after the new organization is created (p. 5). By leveraging synergies, several positive byproducts were produced, including increased revenue, reduced overall costs, combined financial influence, and more robust management (KPMG, 2011).

Growth

Although synergy is a motivating rationale, business activity in recent decades demonstrated M&As are a sought-after strategy for growth (Baldwin, 2012; Saunders, Altinay, & Riordan, 2009; Tikhomirov & Spangler, 2009). Modern organizations are constantly pushed to achieve greater levels of profit each successive year, and in many situations inorganic growth must be pursued to achieve these results (Dickinson, 2013; Dunbar, 2013; George, 2011; Maepa, 2014). Dunbar (2013) further noted M&As allowed companies to grow at a much faster rate than organic growth permitted because outside resources were leveraged. One of the most important reasons for pursuing inorganic growth was the speed of acquiring resources to exploit opportunities, which was not always achieved through internal growth (Thayser, 2014). For these reasons, inorganic growth was a widely-cited rationale for M&As (Chickene, 2013; Dunbar, 2013; Maepa, 2014).

Merger and Acquisition Success and Value

Various methods are used to evaluate the success of an M&A deal, which include goal completion, value increases, and reduced negative outcomes (Bean, 2013; Funk, 2011; Money, 2011). Some authors suggested when the goals set at the beginning of an M&A were achieved, then the transaction could be considered a success (Dickinson, 2013; Money, 2011). Funk (2011) built on this understanding by stating that if an M&A resulted in a greater level of value than the initial costs of the transaction, it was successful. Bean (2013) and Weiner and Hill (2008) shared a different perspective, saying although financial foci were important, success should be measured by limiting negative impacts on employees. Additionally, goal completion and reduced negative outcomes were indicators of success, but many organizations placed a more significant emphasis on increasing value in a purely financial sense (Doseck, 2012; Money, 2011).

The literature revealed that often, the purpose of an M&A was to achieve a more significant level of value for the organization and its shareholders (Baldwin, 2012; Doseck, 2012; Hart & Sherman, 2006; Money, 2011). Despite this, some organizations entered into M&As expecting value to grow, but the transactions failed to increase value (Fairbank, 2006; Galpin & Herndon, 2007; Hopkins, 2008; Quinones-Gonzalez, 2013). Herd and McManuse (2012) expanded on this with data from recent years, which showed 58% of M&A deals created value for their organizations. From a contrasting standpoint, Harding and Rouse (2007) estimated 53% of M&A deals reduced the value of the organizations and 83% failed to deliver any shareholder value. Dickinson (2013) and Stahl and Voigt (2008) acknowledged additional ways to improve a company's value still needed to be explored to mitigate the looming risks.

Merger and Acquisition Failure

Widespread disagreement exists in the literature about the percentage of M&As that fail to obtain success. Research estimated M&As were unable to realize their full potential from as low as 40% to as high as 80% of the time (Dunbar, 2013; Waldman & Javidan, 2009). Other authors found many organizations were unable to achieve successful results more than half of the time (Deutsch & West, 2010; DiGeorgio, 2002; Sher, 2012). Valant (2009) purported failure rates ranged between 60% and 80%, whereas Connell (2010) found failures occurred

50% to 70% of the time. Additional estimates corroborated both Valant (2009) and Connell (2010), stating failures happened 65% of the time (Cartwright & Schoenberg, 2006; DePamphilis, 2009; Doseck, 2012; Marks & Mirvis, 2011). Even with M&As failing as often as they do, companies still utilize M&A as a prominent organizational strategy (De Hoyos, 2013; Tikhomirov & Spangler, 2009; Zollo & Meier, 2008). The literature consistently concluded M&A failure was a substantial problem that continues to plague organizations.

Although failure rates were important to consider, perhaps more paramount was understanding the root causes. De Haldevang (2009), Dunbar (2013), and Schmidt (2008) suggested failure was often the result of complications that arose from human dynamics during an M&A integration process. Many authors agreed poorly coordinated M&A integration processes were the cause of failure (Cho, 2004; de Haldevang, 2009; Hahm et al., 2013; Schmidt, 2008). Money (2011) drilled down further into these causes and insinuated many M&A failures were linked to complexities spurred by mismanagement of personnel during the integration process. Assuming this was true, an opportunity exists to increase the success rates of M&As by better understanding the integration process.

Merger and Acquisition Integration Processes

Doseck (2012) defined integration as "the unique, complex, and often challenging process of combining two or more organizations during a merger or acquisition" (p. 10). The combination of the two companies impacted the entire organization and given its scope, inevitably spurred employee reactions to change (Clayton, 2010; Dickinson, 2013; Knilans, 2009; Sun, 2011). Employees reacted differently to integration processes, with reactions including stress, anxiety, resistance, conflict, job uncertainty, and turnover (Anderson-Ackerman & Anderson, 2010; Bean, 2013; Dickinson, 2013; Geiselmann, 2012; Maepa, 2014; Mao, 2010). Some suggested the integration process was the most essential juncture in the M&A process, the crux of success (Cording, Christmann, & King 2008; Deloitte, 2016; Kale & Singh, 2009; Marks & Mirvis, 2011; Swaminathan, Murshed, & Hulland, 2008). Doseck (2012) and Marks and Mirvis (2011) also declared the M&A integration process was a time when preset expectations would ultimately be tested against the current reality.

With the value of M&As at stake, the literature suggested organizations must plan and prepare carefully before launching an integration process (Doseck, 2012). KPMG (2011) and Roh (2011) proposed when organizations took the time to adequately plan, they aligned various aspects of the two companies that produced a highly synergistic entity. When integration processes were conducted without sufficient preparation and planning, diminished efficiency and performance were experienced by both organizations. The literature further suggested poorly managed integration processes resulted in increased confusion, ambiguity, anxiety, "ambiguous goals, lack of role clarity, and inefficient decision making" (KPMG, 2011, p. 8).

Many of the factors impacting success or failure of an M&A integration connected to how the employees in the organization responded and reacted to the change. Many additional authors suggested achieving success required an understanding of employee feelings and behaviors as well as an understanding of how to engage employees within the complexities of the change efforts (Weber & Drori, 2011; Whitaker, 2012). Dickinson's (2013) study clarified best practices, which included establishing communication goals, showing the benefits of the change, having change be reasonably paced, and "avoiding the strategic, people, external, and operational causes of failure" (p. 81). However, the sheer volume of failed M&A transactions indicated both academic and practical research lacked a comprehensive understanding of the integration process (Weber & Drori, 2011).

Complexity

Cocco (2014) described complexity as a finite capacity to analyze organizational factors because of the quantity and scale of those factors. Ellis (2013) purported change and complexity are two significant challenges prevalent in integration. Dunbar (2013) corroborated this notion and suggested the sheer nature of bringing two organizations together during an integration process significantly increased complexity in the organization. Robinson (2011) stated the level of complexity was driven by variables, such as employees interacting with one another, that produced unpredictable results. Because organizations represent interconnected systems, minor catalysts and provocations had major repercussions throughout the organization (Loorbach & Rotsman, 2009). Gerds et al. (2010) and Vasilaki (2011) believed challenges and problems only worsened as the level of complexity in the organization increased because the integration needed for successful M&As was a highly complex feat. The literature showed integration of two organizations caused levels of complexity and volatility to grow, which created challenges across the organization (Basinger, 2012; Dickinson, 2013; Dunbar, 2013; Jacobs et al., 2013). Authors also affirmed a high level of complexity was associated with organizational change such as the organizations coming together, employee responses to the change, information flow, and frequency of communication (Dunbar, 2013; Jacobs et al., 2013; Jansson, 2013; Robinson, 2011).

Change

At the most basic level, M&A integration processes are examples of large-scale change, which inevitably impacts the entire organization (Dunbar, 2013; Hahm et al., 2013; Quinones-Gonzalez, 2013). As such, a more in-depth understanding of the impact of change benefited those charged with managing integration processes. Maepa (2014) contended change was difficult for employees because it caused disruption and a battle between people trying to maintain the status quo and those trying to advance the organization. Armstrong (2011) further suggested change naturally created disruption in the workplace and instigated several reactions from employees. Nesterkin (2013) stated change infringed upon employee autonomy. KPMG (2011) found large-scale disruptions caused productivity declines upwards of 25% to 50%. The literature suggested when employees experienced change, even if the change was executed perfectly, natural resistance still formed (Balle, 2008; Dickens, 2012). Ellis (2013) and George (2011) acknowledged resistance could cause failures during the integration process.

When looking at an integration process through the lens of change, it is no surprise integrations have high failure rates. Change management research suggested over 70% of organizational changes end up failing when implemented (Burke, 2013; Jansson, 2013). Cope (2003) estimated an even higher failure rate for change, stating change endeavors failed 80% to 90% of the time. Conversely, research by Isern and Pung (2007) indicated that among the executives surveyed, 38% found their change initiatives were successful. In both cases, the rate of unsuccessful change was high, which indicated the need for increased knowledge to improve the probability of success (Dickens, 2012; Jansson, 2013; Quinones-Gonzalez, 2013; Smith, 2002). The change literature suggested a key to increasing the success rate of change was the organization's ability to more effectively manage uncertainty (Armstrong, 2011).

Uncertainty

Bordia et al. (2004) defined uncertainty as the "lack of knowledge about current or future events" (p. 512). Cocco (2014) contended uncertainty resulted from insufficient information to inform judgments about the future. Mahajan (2011) confirmed when the future was unknown and highly unpredictable, uncertainty grew for employees. Galpin and Herndon (2014) asserted that if given the option, employees would prefer to know about bad circumstances than to be uncertain about all circumstances. Basinger (2012) explained uncertainty must be reduced to allow employees to operate effectively in the new organization. Ralston (2014) contended if uncertainty was left unaddressed, organizations lost efficiency and effectiveness. However, Guindon (2013) offered that if actions were taken to mitigate uncertainty, there were better chances for M&A integration success.

Types of Uncertainty

Mann (2011) acknowledged additional research is needed regarding the specific types of uncertainty present in an organization undergoing a change and how each type impacted the workforce. Bordia et al. (2004) developed a model that explored three overarching types of uncertainty: strategic uncertainty, structural uncertainty, and job-related uncertainty. The purpose of the model was to explain uncertainty amidst change efforts to a greater degree. Within the model, strategic uncertainty was described as "uncertainty regarding organizational level issues," which often focused on the rationale for the change, where the organization was heading, and the shifting environment of the organization (Bordia et al., 2004, p. 510). Strategic uncertainty involved informational, environmental, and technological uncertainty by limiting available information, changing the working landscape, and altering existing aspects of operations (Bean, 2013; Bordia et al., 2004; Mann, 2011; Ragatz, Handfield, & Petersen, 2002; Ralston, 2014; Van den Bos, 2009).

Structural and job-related uncertainties were the next two pieces of the model. Structural uncertainty looked at the impact uncertainty had on day-to-day operations, including the "reporting structures and functions of different work units" (Bordia et al., 2004, p. 510). Structural uncertainty included informational, environmental, and project uncertainty, which all attended to the shifting organizational conditions occurring because of integration processes (Bean, 2013; Bordia et al., 2004; Cocco, 2014; Grover & Malhotra, 2003; Mann, 2011; Ralston, 2014; Van den Bos, 2009).

Job-related uncertainty focused on how uncertainty plagued employees at an individual level, often altering job security and promotional opportunities, and prompting changes to specific job roles (Bordia et al., 2004). Job-related uncertainty consisted of informational, personal, technological, career, and project uncertainties as each of these areas dealt directly with the employee and his or her relationship to the organization, the integration process, and other employees within the company (Bordia et al., 2004; Bos, 2007; Cocco, 2014; Mahajan, 2011; Mann, 2011; Van den Bos, 2009). Table 1 outlines the types of uncertainty and associated challenges.

Table 1

Uncertainty Synthesis Matrix

Uncertainty	Type of Uncertainty	Challenges
Informational	Strategic, Structural, Job-Related	Not enough information for effective decision-making
Personal	Job-Related	Lack of clarity about employee and manager roles in an organization
Environmental	Strategic, Structural	Changing organizational conditions that create unpredictability
Technological	Strategic, Job-Related	Changes to products or services with subsequent impacts on other goods and services
Career	Job-Related	No understanding of role or long-term job
Project	Structural, Job-Related	No understanding about how an employee will contribute to the project

Note. Adapted from Bean (2013), Bordia et al. (2004), Bos

(2007), Cocco (2014), Mahajan (2011), Mann (2011), Ragatz et al. (2002), Ralston (2014), and Van den Bos (2009).

In a practical sense, uncertainty manifested itself in many forms during a change process, including role confusion, job insecurity, and concerns about benefits (Burke, 2013; Mann, 2011; Van den Bos, 2009). The literature further suggested when integration occurs, a company assumed a new identity, which resulted in a departure from its old culture (Armstrong, 2011; Whitaker, 2012). As a result, employees often mourned the loss of the old culture and struggled with uncertainty about norms, job expectations, traditions, and the workplace environment (Busch, 2011; Cameron & Quinn, 2005; Knilans, 2009; Saunders et al., 2009). Burke (2013) and Mann (2011) suggested change increased uncertainty because the new organization removed control from employees and these dynamics were further compounded when employees were not involved with implementing the change. The literature suggested the impact of change and more specifically the uncertainty created during the change process should not be underestimated (Ralston, 2014).

Impacts of Uncertainty on the Employee

Uncertainty negatively impacted organizations and resulted in productivity losses, employee turnover, and diminishing market share (PwC, 2011). Galpin and Herndon (2014) further noted when uncertainty ran rampant across the organization, employees lost focus on organizational objectives and turned their attention to how the change was impacting them personally. The longer a major change took for its completion, the more uncertainty impacted employees and eroded confidence (Galpin & Herndon, 2014; Mahajan, 2011).

Employees had more tension with the organization when uncertainty was high (Khan, 2013; Thau, Aquino, & Wittek, 2007). Venema (2015) supported this assertion, stating anxiety grew for employees when they were uncertain about their future with the organization. Complementary research suggested as uncertainty increased, stress also rose, causing employees to try and reduce the uncertainty (Khan, 2013; Malik & Kabiraj, 2010; Venema, 2015). The rise in stress and anxiety was often attributed to the attitude employees had toward the change and new organization. Whitaker (2012) acknowledged uncertainty could be a potent force for driving negative mindsets toward the integration. Employees fell into a state of hopelessness when they felt negatively about their futures, which led to depression (Mahajan, 2011; Miranda, Fontes, & Marroquin, 2008). Mahajan (2011) shared that as negative feelings abound in response to the integration process, employees felt a heightened need to reduce uncertainty. The literature revealed effectively managed information could help during large-scale change and integration processes.

Middle Managers

Doseck (2012) and Dunbar (2013) suggested that although executives and frontline employees were critical to the success of M&A integration processes, middle managers had a greater role in influencing organizational performance. Sanders and Frenkel (2011) described middle management as the buffer between top leadership and frontline employees, as they oversaw various organizational activities. Ferry (2010) further specified the role of middle management was to guide daily work duties and tasks of frontline employees, as directed by top management. Allan and Cianni (2011) and Dickinson (2013) contended middle managers were imperative to an M&A integration process, as they advised employees on changes to their roles and provided daily direction. Paruchuri, Nerker, and Hambrick (2006) confirmed when employees were disturbed by change efforts, manager intervention increased the chances for M&A integration success.

The literature was clear that managers improved the organization's chances for integration success by actively working to reduce uncertainty for employees (Galpin & Herndon, 2014; Guindon, 2013; Knilans, 2009; Mann, 2011). Oreg and Berson (2011) and Maepa (2014) conferred that during times of major change, employees looked to leaders to help reduce uncertainty. Balle's (2008) research confirmed employees went to their direct supervisors about 80% of the time when questions arose during an integration process. Armstrong (2011) argued managers who oversaw an integration process needed to reduce uncertainty by answering questions to more effectively facilitate the change and bolster stability. Jarrard (2014) reinforced Armstrong (2011), advising that by better understanding what was happening with the change, employees were free to refocus their efforts on work instead of worrying about an uncertain future. However, many managers were ill-prepared to effectively fill this role. Dean and Cianni (2011) acknowledged managers needed training to learn to manage integration processes and more effectively limit negative impacts on the M&A; however, their research did not make specific recommendations (Gallego-Toledo, 2015). De Cremer et al. (2010) suggested an opportunity for additional research to determine the most effective ways to minimize and manage uncertainty.

Employee Reaction to Uncertainty

Whitaker (2012) contended that during an M&A integration process, major change rippled through the organization psychologically impacting employees along the way. Naturally, employees would be concerned about how they would be personally impacted. Bean (2013) found employees commonly used emotions and feelings to describe their perspective of the integration processes. An employee could have a variety of reactions to a change in the organization, which included "anxiety, anger, fear, enthusiasm, and apprehension" (Erwin & Garman, 2010, p. 43).

Gallego-Toledo (2015) and Outlay (2008) both agreed when change violated the expectations of the employee, they felt betrayed by the organization. Depending on the reaction from the employee, the integration process provoked "denial, anxious thoughts, and emotions or outright shock that the change is taking place" (Knilans, 2009, p. 6). When integration processes were prolonged, employee routines were disrupted leading to frustration, anxiety, anger, and limited motivation (Nesterkin, 2013; Wallis et al., 2006). Kiefer (2005) believed these behaviors led to organizational issues such as poor climate, inappropriate management, role uncertainty, reduced motivation, and ignored policies and incentives. Negativity also had a perverse effect on the workforce by lowering morale and potentially performance along with it (Fink, 2010). When employees had a negative perspective of the change, concerns about the integration process manifested itself through their behavior.

The literature showed employee behaviors were a significant determinant of the success of an M&A. When employees viewed the integration process as negative, their behavior became counterproductive (Bean, 2013; Dickinson, 2013; Gilley et al., 2009). "Imposing new behaviors and eliminating old ones" created friction and resistance among a workforce concerned about their role and freedoms, which caused turnover and a rise in dissatisfaction (Nesterkin, 2013, p. 574). Bean (2013) discussed other negative behaviors employees often exemplified, including "emotional withdrawal and self-absorption, withdrawn support, reduced effort, resistance towards the integration process and transition requirements, hostility, distracted activities, voiced negative opinions, fault-finding, and premature turnover" (p. 153). Whitaker (2012) warned if the behaviors did not solicit a response from the organization, they grew in scale or intensity, creating unintended consequences for the organization.

Stress and Anxiety

Organizational change often increased the amount of anxiety and stress felt by the employees (Bean, 2013; Carola, 2010; El Hag, 2003; Maepa, 2014; Nikolau, Vakola, & Bourantas, 2011; PwC, 2011). Dickinson (2013) and Maepa (2014) confirmed that as uncertainty grew, employees became anxious from a lack of knowledge about their current situation. Miranda et al. (2008) said the uncertainty felt by employees about their future may lead to depression and anxiety. Anxiety was induced by major changes within the organization because employees needed to alter their "knowledge, skills, work behaviors, and relationships" (Baldwin, 2012, p. 10).

Stress could be interpreted as employees' natural response to a highly irregular event (Ahmad, Zia-ur-Rehman, & Rashid, 2011). Stress materialized when change and high uncertainty impacted the employee, and the natural reaction was to look for information to reduce this stress (Khan, 2013; Romano, 2014). Research determined failure to provide employees sufficient information increased uncertainty, which led to higher levels of stress and anxiety (Geiselmann, 2012; Venema, 2015). De Croon, Sluiter, Kuijer, and Frings-Dresen (2005) and De Lange, Taris, Kompier, Houtman, and Bongers (2002) confirmed the changing circumstances of integration created an abundance of unnecessary information thrown at employees, which incurred high levels of stress.

Appelbaum et al. (2007) and Maepa (2014) concurred stress and anxiety contributed to integration failure. Stress and anxiety were provoked by the integration process because it fundamentally changed the organization (Dickinson, 2013; Maepa, 2014). Stress could be brought on during the integration process from a lack of communication, limited trust, new roles, and tight integration deadlines (Armstrong, 2011; Clayton, 2010; Oreg, 2006; Roberson, 2004). Research confirmed employees engaged in M&A activity had higher levels of stress, which caused negativity and resulted in the failure of the change (Carola, 2010; Cartwright & Schoenberg, 2006; Clayton, 2010). Bean (2013) postulated anxiety and stress crippled integration processes, and when left unresolved, they invited more pronounced displays of counterproductive behavior such as resistance.

Resistance

Resistance developed from employees' feelings, emotions, and reactions to the integration process and its impact on each person in the workforce (Anderson-Ackerman & Anderson, 2010). Resistance refers to emotional reactions instigated when they people perceive a change not fulfilling their needs (Anderson-Ackerman & Anderson, 2010). From a different viewpoint, resistance could be understood as revolting against the changes in the organization (Bercovitz & Feldman, 2008; Cameron & Quinn, 2005; Danişman, 2010). Erkama (2010) and Stensaker and Langley (2009) acknowledged that at its core, resistance was an attempt by employees to keep existing condition intact during a large-scale change. Anderson (2012) and Ishii (2006) also found uncertainty instigated resistance among the workforce. George (2011) stated that when employees were opposed to the change or did not feel it was in their best interest, they could resort to forming resistance against both the change and the organization.

Baldwin (2012) noted resistance developed from not having the necessary amount of information needed to effectively function during the integration process. Danişman (2010) and Levay (2010) also believed a lack of understanding about the integration process allowed resistance to be inflamed by employee frustrations and negative perspectives of the change. The research suggested resistance grew when no vision existed, trust was minimal, and employee engagement was low (Gallego-Toledo, 2015; Maurer, 2003; Nesterkin, 2013; Oreg, 2006). Deviant behaviors initiated by resistance could be highly pernicious because employees influenced how much resistance appeared across the organization (Ford, Ford, & D'Amelio, 2008; Furst-Holloway & Cable, 2008).

An integration process also directly impacts employee value and belief systems and efforts to handle these challenges led to resistance and change failure (George, 2011). Resistance was expected from employees impacted by change, especially if the integration did not properly account for employee needs (Anderson-Ackerman & Anderson, 2010; Baldwin, 2012; George, 2011; Gerds et al., 2010; Saunders et al., 2009). Employee resistance against organizational change was well established in the literature, which suggested resistance was one of the primary causes of failure (Ellis, 2013; Erkama, 2010; Erwin & Garman, 2010; Zoller & Fairhurst, 2007). Jacobs et al. (2013) cautioned when resistance runs rampant, it delayed the integration process and organizations incurred significant costs along the way.

Conflict

When the organization remained chaotic and unorganized during an integration process, uncertainty spurred conflict (Bowditch & Buono, 2004; Kulp, 2012). De Dreu and Gelfand (2008) confirmed issues that stirred conflict included different interests, unique values, or disparate thoughts about the organization. Barki and Pinsonneault (2005) noted conflict could also be sparked when a result of the integration process was a perceived loss of control. Additionally, when communication was not utilized to resolve conflict, issues drastically grew in intensity and scale (Arendt, Priem, & Ndofor, 2005; Ihidero, 2011). Sun (2011) asserted conflict had the potential to inhibit the success of integration efforts.

Ihidero (2011) affirmed conflict could not be avoided and would occur no matter the preparation, so the challenge was how to minimize the damage. Mao (2010) believed manager-employee conflict was inevitable during an integration process and the resolution to these conflicts impacted the organization. Although conflict could be a productive force in an organization, often it was left unresolved which spurred greater conflicts in the process (De Alwis, 2013; Rahim, 2001). Mao (2010) offered that conflicts resulted when misunderstandings and disagreements escalated without any intervention. Jacobs et al. (2013) suggested conflict that erupted in the workforce lowered overall work satisfaction. Without an open workplace atmosphere and trust among the workforce, conflict continued to spoil the organization from inside (Bakar, Mustaffa, & Mohamad, 2009; Clayton, 2010). Lakshman (2011) remarked that when trust was not evident during an integration process, conflict went from a possibility to an inevitable outcome.

Job Uncertainty and Turnover

During an integration process, employees had increased uncertainty about their organizational role because job responsibilities could be changed and altered (Kohut, 2010). Job uncertainty became a major issue and was characterized by financial and career insecurity as well as a loss of identity and community (Balle, 2008; Geiselmann, 2012). Job uncertainty was also described as apprehension felt by employees when they were unsure about the future of their job (Cheng & Chan, 2008; Vander Elst et al., 2010).

Uncertainty was also intricately connected to turnover

in the organization (Bean, 2013; El Hag, 2003). Turnover negatively impacted an organization because resources were expended to recruit and train new employees and complete any interim work (Krug, 2009; Maepa, 2014). Turnover could be caused by anxiety, poor communication practices, nominal organizational identification, and overall frustration with the integration process (Appelbaum, Gandell, Shapiro, Belisle, & Hoeven, 2000; Maepa, 2014; Weber & Drori, 2011; Whitaker, 2012). Additionally, the relationship between management and employees influenced turnover and poor relationships caused employees to leave the organization (Arons, 2010; Cicero, Pierro, & Van Knippenberg, 2010). Tannous and Cheng (2007) asserted turnover also impacted the highest echelons of management with successful integration processes resulting in 25% turnover compared to a turnover rate of 67% in failed transactions. Organizations with high turnover could also have poor performance and productivity (Ooghe, Van Laere, & De Langhe, 2006; Roh, 2011; Steelman, 2009). Integration processes altered the productivity of employees, caused unintended turnover of employees, and impacted the organization's ability to achieve success (Alexandris, Petmezas, & Travlos, 2010; Clayton, 2010; Guindon, 2013).

Ways to Reduce Uncertainty

As previously established, when a major change impacted an employee's job and workplace, uncertainty increased (Burke, 2013). If employees concentrated on the uncertainty, they began to feel overwhelmed by the change, thus losing focus on job responsibilities (PwC, 2011). Basinger (2012) asserted to get employees comfortable in their new environments, it was critical to actively work to reduce uncertainty that permeated from major change. Jarrard (2014) supported this notion, noting that clearing up uncertainty in the organization could be highly beneficial for employees seriously affected by the organizational change. Van den Bos and Lind (2002) suggested employees always tried to regulate uncertainty when it appeared in the organization. Vazirani and Mohapatra (2012) confirmed managers were essential in confronting uncertainty and helped employees cope with the change.

Organizational Communication

When an integration process altered the current organization, strategic communication was critical to foster change (Jian, 2011; Kohut, 2010; Quinones-Gonzalez, 2013; Skalik, Barabasz, & Belz, 2002). Communication was defined as the transfer of information from a sender to receiver with a focus was usually on tasks, results, outcomes, and goals (Busch, 2011; Dickens, 2012; Knilans, 2009). When employees were hesitant about the change, communication became a significant factor in determining the success or failure of the integration process (Appelbaum et al., 2007; Doseck, 2012; Geiselmann, 2012; Kohut, 2010; Maepa, 2014; Saunder et al., 2009). Additional authors supported this claim, saying communication was one of the most important elements to achieving success during an integration process and ultimately promoting successful organizational change (Dickens, 2012; Kohut, 2010; Muller, 2006; Towers Perrin, 2003; Vazirani & Mohapatra, 2012). Ellis (2013), Jarrard (2014), and Nguyen and Kleiner (2003) suggested poorly executed communication caused failure during the integration process. Integration success was driven by how engaged the employees were with the change, which was generally dependent upon organizational communication (Jones, Watson, Gardner, & Gallois, 2004).

When undergoing integration, organizations needed to strategically utilize communication to send information to their employees (Balle, 2008; Dickinson, 2013; Malik & Kabiraj, 2010; PwC, 2011; Vander Elst et al., 2010). Khan (2013) contended employees needed communication to function and reduce uncertainty during times of massive change like integration. Maepa (2014) warned without communication or any formalized strategy to share information, uncertainty rose. Middle managers were key to delivering appropriate and timely communication. The literature suggested when looking for answers to questions regarding an integration process, employees went to middle managers because they were communication beacons in the organization (Balle, 2008; Bardwick, 2008; Towers Perrin, 2005). Lehman and DuFrene (2008) estimated 60-80% of the average manager's time was spent on communication issues. Additionally, the literature proposed communication was enhanced through face-to-face interactions with managers and communication enhanced performance by 5-10% (Quach, 2013; Wagner & Harter, 2006). The literature further suggested when correctly implemented, communication enhanced employee engagement, lessened anxiety, improved productivity and decision-making, and delivered higher levels of performance (Arons, 2010; Larbi-Apau & Moseley, 2009; Quach, 2013; Venema, 2015; Weber, Rachman-Moore, & Tarba, 2012). Basinger (2012) noted manager focus on employee information needs allowed employees to better understand the goals of the integration process and support its ongoing efforts.

Trust

An essential aspect of reducing uncertainty and realizing a successful integration process was trust (Appelbaum et al., 2007; Kavanagh & Ashkanasy, 2006; Saunders et al., 2009). Trust was described as how people defined their relationships with others and as the integration process evolved, trust continued to be a critical factor for the organization (Dickens, 2012; Quach, 2013). DePamphilis (2014) acknowledged integration processes increased uncertainty about one's personal circumstances and the new company's future, which undercut existing trust in an organization and crippled the integration process if not carefully managed. Employees given ample information about the integration process had higher levels of trust, meaning employees were far more open to the change (Dickens, 2012; Nikandrou, Papalexandris, & Bourantas, 2000). Colquitt and Salam (2009) asserted the success of an integration process related to trust because the number of organizational advantages it yielded such as innovation, creativity, performance, commitment, communication, and quality relationships with employees.

Trust impacted the integration process because it was intertwined with so many elements of the organization (Dickens, 2012). As cultures were integrating, trust was an effective stimulant for collaboration across the organization (Vazirani & Mohapatra, 2012). In-person interactions and participation were effective strategies for developing trust (Quach, 2013). Ihidero (2011) and Lakshman (2011) noted trust was also a highly effective tool that combatted disruptive conflict in the workplace. Trust in one's manager was linked to the success of the integration process and the consistency of a manager's words and actions were paramount for employees to establish trust (Clayton, 2010; Dickinson, 2013; Kotter, 2007; Muller, 2006; Nikolau et al., 2011). Organizational trust was also impacted by communication in the organization and as communication improved, trust grew (Dickinson, 2013; Muller, 2006; Quach, 2013). Additionally, trust decreased stress, curtailed negative attitudes, promoted commitment, instilled cooperation with employees, limited turnover, and improved performance (Weber et al., 2014).

Fairness

Lind and Van den Bos (2002) and Mann (2011) concurred fairness and fair processes were essential for employees who operated and functioned with the many different uncertain elements of the integration process. Fairness could be procedural and defined through organizational policies or interactional dealing directly with treatment of employees (Brockner, Wiesenfeld, & Diekmann, 2009). A core need for employees was fairness, which was especially important during times of massive organizational change (Anderson-Ackerman & Anderson, 2010). Fair processes highlighted the fairness of the organization and expectations of fair practices in the future (De Cremer & Sedikides, 2008). Fair processes were linked to how employees reacted emotionally and allowed employees a consistent way to gauge themselves in the organization (De Cremer et al., 2010; Smollan & Sayers, 2009).

Inevitably, integration processes had various challenges,

which caused employees to be attentive to organizational fairness (De Cremer et al., 2010; Mann, 2011; Lind & Van den Bos, 2002; Thau, Bennett, Mitchell, & Marrs, 2009). Employee attention to fairness was heightened by increased uncertainty in the organization (De Cremer et al., 2010; De Cremer & Sedikides, 2005; Lind & Van den Bos, 2002; Mann, 2011). Employees actively pursued information related to fairness because at its core, it helps reduce uncertainty (Lind & Van den Bos, 2002; Mann, 2011; Pyc, 2011). Thau, Aquino, and Wittek (2007) claimed depending upon the employee's perspective, fairness could be viewed as either just or unfair. If employees feel they were treated unfairly, they reacted adversely, especially when uncertainty was high (Pyc, 2011; Thau et al., 2009). However, by managing fairness and fair processes, managers in the organization worked to reduce uncertainty and build trust (De Cremer & Sedikides, 2008; Mann, 2011; Pyc, 2011). Colquitt, Greenberg, and Zapta-Phelan (2005) alleged when fairness was to the satisfaction of employees, there was a stronger chance they supported the integration process and organization.

Engagement

Maepa (2014) described engagement as a powerful tool for encouraging and guiding employees through the integration process. Armstrong (2011) noted the success of M&As required employees to be engaged in the integration process. Dickinson (2013) thought the integration affected every employee, which directly influenced engagement and turnover. Multiple authors suggested high amounts of uncertainty caused by the integration process reduced employee engagement and caused a loss of control for employees (Basinger, 2012; KPMG, 2011; Mann,

2011). However, highly engaged employees steered integration results to a much greater degree than employees not involved (Weber & Drori, 2011).

Weber and Drori (2011) further affirmed higher engagement was associated with a greater chance of realizing integration expectations. Multiple authors proposed higher levels of engagement improved commitment, reduced uncertainty, and developed culture (Gallego-Toledo, 2015; Whitaker, 2012). Gallego-Toledo (2015) expanded on this viewpoint, saying employee engagement during integration processes led to several positive effects such as "increased morale, job satisfaction, organizational commitment levels, and reduced resistance to change" (p. 66-67). Managers also increased engagement by utilizing a strong vision and high levels of trust, which effectively engaged employees and increased commitment (Gallego-Toledo, 2015; Maepa, 2014). Furthermore, engaged employees were 20% more productive and often achieved higher levels of profitability (Gallup Consulting, 2011; Sengupta & Ramadoss, 2011).

Commitment

Commitment to change was demonstrated through employee willingness to support and implement change (Dickens, 2012; Fedor et al., 2006). However, if not managed carefully, major change across the organization potentially impacted commitment and impeded change (Erwin & Garman, 2010; Seo & Hill, 2005). For these reasons, employee commitment was essential to the success of an integration process and the organization needed to make every effort to instill commitment in their workforce to achieve integration objectives (Able, 2007;

Steele, 2014). Waldman and Javidan (2009) stressed the importance of employees staying committed to a direction for the integration process or uncertainty grew and became increasingly detrimental to change efforts.

Employee commitment influenced the engagement and motivation needed to implement major changes happening during an integration process (Leroy, Palanski, & Simons, 2012). Commitment and trust could also be enhanced through communication (Colquitt & Salam, 2009; Guindon, 2013; Maepa, 2014; Morgan & Zeffane, 2003). Managers had the distinct capability of affecting commitment because of their unique relationship between upper management and frontline employees (Clayton, 2010; Dickinson, 2013; Guindon, 2013; Gupta & Sharma, 2008).

Planning

Planning for integration was essential because it detailed a set of strategies to drive success and crystalized the company direction (Knilans, 2009). Galpin and Herndon (2014) stated problems with integration processes were not solely from poor implementation, but many times resulted from a lack of plans and strategies that effectively facilitated the transition. Whitaker (2012) understood that perfection may not be attained during implementation, but rather the goal was to set strategies that coordinated the success of the integration process to the greatest degree possible. Dickinson (2013) suggested a good plan entailed timelines, actions, and outcomes for consolidating the two separate companies into a single entity. Multiple authors pointed out an integration plan dramatically increased the chances for integration success (David, 2009; Doseck, 2012; Kotter, 2007; KPMG, 2011; Papadakis, 2007). Dickinson (2013) and Venema (2015) recalled with the costs for M&As, it became essential to limit the possibility of failure by adequately planning for success.

Leading experts suggested clear plans helped limit uncertainty by providing a tangible roadmap for the integration process that could be followed by employees (PwC, 2014). Doseck (2012) and Tikhomirov and Spangler (2009) concluded plans needed to be formed to guide the integration process and provide stability, but also the integration process required some level of adaptability to respond to real-time organizational conditions. Accordingly, managers needed to develop effective plans that could be altered appropriately when the integration process required a course correction (Chickene, 2013; David, 2009; Dickinson, 2013). KPMG (2011) forewarned when organizations did not effectively plan for the integration process, they opened themselves up to a plethora of problems such as unclear goals, unknown job responsibilities, and poor competencies for making decisions.

Decision-Making

Decision-making was acknowledged as a challenge within organizations, especially during times of major change (Armstrong, 2011). Organizational decision-making had widespread outcomes because one decision rippled across the organization and had lasting impacts (Reider, 2011). Two decision-making events would never be the same because of variations in the environments and circumstances for each decision (Reider, 2011). These circumstances became magnified when a lack of information, short time frame, and resistance obscured organizational decisions (Baldwin, 2012; Mann, 2011).

Chickene (2013) noted the sheer speed and complexity of an M&A integration process required the organization's decision-making capabilities to be efficient and timely. Decision-making as an activity was incredibly complicated because it entailed accounting for the vast number of variables and unknown factors that influenced each decision (Reider, 2011). Authors believed communication throughout the entire organization improved decision-making and helped employees cope with changing circumstances (Arons, 2010; Larbi-Apau & Moseley, 2009; Liang, Ndofor, Priem, & Picken, 2010; Quach, 2013). Managers who supported decision-making and reduced the complexity of decisions throughout the integration process dramatically improved the organization's capacity to make and execute decisions (Armstrong, 2011; Mann, 2011; Zollo & Singh, 2004). Decision-making during an integration process was driven from within the culture and could be improved with appropriate planning (Deloitte, 2009; KPMG, 2011).

Vision

One variable that had a lasting impact on change was the vision and how it was shared among the organization (Skalik et al., 2002). Knilans (2009) described the organization vision as the desired future and end state. A clear vision defined the expectations of the integration process and created a shared vision for the workforce (Dickinson, 2013; Funk, 2011). Waldman and Javidan (2009) warned that without a vision, employees lost focus of M&A goals. This was why M&A failure could often be traced back lack of a clear vision for the integration process (Armstrong, 2011; KPMG, 2011; Nguyen & Kleiner, 2003).

Basinger (2012) and Funk (2011) confirmed having a vision reduced uncertainty because it provided employees with a better understanding of what the integration process entailed.

An M&A integration process needed a vision to focus staff and to effectively manage the transition within the organization (Armstrong, 2011). Vision alleviated strain by letting employees keep their attention on the future and find their way through the change (Armstrong, 2011; Knilans, 2009). Middle managers were crucial to align employees around a mutual vision and clearly communicate stability during the M&A integration process (Clayton, 2010; Dickinson, 2013; Knilans, 2009; Nikolau et al., 2011). Maurer (2003) and Waldman and Javidan (2009) took it a step further and said when the organization allowed employees to assist in the creation of the vision, commitment rose and resistance declined. Clayton (2010) and Strange and Mumford (2002) confirmed a clear vision could be a potent tool for bringing together many diverse groups and teams during the chaos of an M&A integration process. David (2009) also emphasized a vision was an effective tool during the integration process when correctly implemented.

Culture

Vazirani and Mohapatra (2012) defined culture as "the informal values, norms, and beliefs" that influenced the way employees and teams "interact with each other and with people outside the organization" (p. 33). Alternatively, Doseck (2012) illustrated culture as the "accepted norms of an organization that is a result of shared experiences" (p. 34). Additional authors agreed culture encompassed the values, norms, and actions of employees (Appelbaum et al., 2009; Busch, 2011;

Cameron & Quinn, 2011). In this sense, culture was created through daily employee actions and interactions, and espoused how the organization functioned (Busch, 2011; PwC, 2011). With this understanding, culture was an effective tool to reduce uncertainty because it created stability for employees in establishing shared practices and operational standards (Saunders et al., 2009; Yukl, 2006).

Bringing two cultures together during an M&A integration process was about creating a functioning and productive working relationship with the hopes of improving chances for successful integration (Bean, 2013; Whitaker, 2012). Culture needed to be a critical consideration during the integration process because it was linked to performance, commitment, decision-making, communication, trust, engagement, and the work environment (Armstrong, 2011; Cameron & Quinn, 2005; Deloitte, 2009; Knilans, 2009; Vazirani & Mohapatra, 2012; Whitaker, 2012). Aon Hewitt (2011), Doseck (2012), and Gallego-Toledo (2015) offered the combination of two previously distinct cultures was one of the most difficult components of M&A integration, and poorly executed efforts often led to slowed execution and failed transactions. Integrating two cultures was the managers' responsibility and essential to improving the possibility for successful M&A integration (Bean, 2013; Deloitte, 2009).

Routines and Norms

Norms were a guiding force within the organization because they dictated employee behavior and influenced culture (Appelbaum et al., 2009; Busch, 2011; Vazirani & Mohapatra, 2012). Related to norms, routines also had the potential to aid or hinder the integration process (Chu, 2012). Allatta and Singh (2011) attested that employees follow their routines and norms unless the change created uncertainty about how they should perform. Whitaker (2012) explained in the absence of norms and routines to follow, employees became less productive and supportive of the integration process. Unprofitable routines and norms delivered lackluster performance, so during an integration process attention needed to be paid to the realignment or development of constructive norms (Chu, 2012; Whitaker, 2012).

Chu (2012) and George (2011) acknowledged managers face a major challenge to change behaviors during an integration process, which was especially difficult because it confronted employee norms and routines. When an M&A integration occurred, routines needed to change, which proved difficult because of the massive impact they had on day-to-day operations (Allatta & Singh, 2011). Whitaker (2012) confirmed without specific plans to help guide major change, employee routines were altered, which created chaos and confusion for daily operations. When managers focused on changing norms and routines, it supported integration (Whitaker, 2012). Additionally, M&A activity provoked the loss of current routines in favor of new routines (Balle, 2008). However, Whitaker (2012) purported when employees and managers were proactive with establishing norms, they stayed focused and productive throughout the integration process.

Group Identification

Massive change within an organization had many unpronounced side effects, such as lowering employee identification with their organization (Jacobs et al., 2013). Balle (2008) noted employees experienced myriad losses during major changes, which included lost income, rights, positions, conveniences, peers, traditions, and group identification. Research also showed threatening employee identity and losing one's identity within the organization was often caused by high levels of uncertainty during the integration process (Geiselmann, 2012; Stillman & Baumeister, 2009). Whitaker (2012) remarked the typical employee responses to integration uncertainty included identity loss, reduced control, fear, and ultimately challenging the change. Mahajan (2011) also noted as the integration process occurred, changes to careers impacted employee identity.

Group identification within the organization was critical to reducing uncertainty (Cicero et al., 2010; Hogg, 2007; Mahajan, 2011). People by nature need some level of social contact, which made group identification so important (Basinger, 2012). When employees identified with the organization, there was a higher probability they would be satisfied with the integration process (Creasy, Stull, & Peck, 2009). Managers also contributed to how employees identified with the organization (Arons, 2010; Balle, 2008). Chickene (2013) illustrated this sentiment by stating employees consistently engaged in the change contributed to the goals of the integration process. Arons (2010) affirmed the ability to identify with the organization came from various interactions, social connections, and communication patterns employees had within the organization.

Summary

An M&A integration process and its associated high level of uncertainty inundated many managers despite their experience (Galpin & Herndon, 2014). Gerds et al. (2010) and Ulrich, Wieseke, and Vam Dick (2005) confirmed managers handled an M&A integration process at least one time during their careers, which was alarming considering most managers were not trained for an event of this magnitude. Smith (2002) noticed circumstances that invited failure included a lack of training, poor skill competency, and counterproductive manager actions. Knowing this, managers were increasingly demanding training to increase their effectiveness (Dean & Cianni, 2011). Additionally, managers needed to mitigate the possibility for hindering the success of an integration process and be proficient in handling the change and resistance that may spawn from it (Gallego-Toledo, 2015; KPMG, 2011).

Although managers were typically prepared to handle the technical aspects of their job, the complexity of an M&A integration process added disruptions that were uncomfortable (Appelo, 2010). On top of the technical aspects of their jobs, managers were also called upon to take on ancillary roles and responsibilities during an integration process (Ellis, 2013; Tikhomirov & Spangler, 2009). Given this reality, managers were sometimes ill-equipped to handle the challenges integration (Allan & Cianni, 2011; Ullrich et al., 2005). This study aimed to provide greater insight into how middle managers perceived organizations manage job-related, structural, and strategic uncertainty during an M&A integration process. The research further explored middle managers' perceptions about what strategies were perceived to be effective and ineffective to manage job-related, structural, and strategic uncertainty during an M&A integration process. Finally, the study worked to identify the strategies that middle managers recommended to manage job-related, structural and strategic uncertainty during an M&A integration process.

This chapter provided a review of literature pertaining to M&As, which included success and failure rates and the complexity of integration. Chapter III describes the methodology, design, sample, and procedures for conducting this research.

CHAPTER III: METHODOLOGY

Chapter III describes the methodology utilized for this study. It starts with a restatement of the purpose and research questions. The remainder of this chapter outlines the research design, population, sample, instrumentation, data collection and analysis procedures, and potential limitations of the study.

Purpose Statement

The purpose of this qualitative study was to explore middle managers' perceptions about how organizations managed job-related, structural, and strategic uncertainty during a merger and acquisition (M&A) integration process. Furthermore, this research investigated what strategies middle managers perceived effective and ineffective for managing job-related, structural, and strategic uncertainty during an M&A integration process. Finally, this study worked to identify the strategies middle managers recommended to manage job-related, structural, and strategic uncertainty during an M&A integration process.

Research Questions

The following research questions served as a basis for this study:

1. How did middle managers perceive organizations managed job-related, structural, and strategic uncertainty during an M&A integration process?

2. What strategies did middle managers perceive to be effective for managing job-related, structural, and strategic uncertainty during an M&A integration process?

3. What strategies did middle managers perceive to be effective for managing job-related, structural, and strategic uncertainty during an M&A integration process?

4. What recommendations did middle managers make for managing job-related, structural, and strategic uncertainty during an M&A integration process?

Research Design

After considering of the complexity of the M&A integration processes, a qualitative research design was best suited for this study. Qualitative research was defined as "research that produces descriptive data... [through] people's own written or spoken words and observable behavior" (Taylor, Bogdan, & DeVault, 2015, p. 4). Patton (2002) reinforced this sentiment, praising qualitative studies for their ability to garner depth and details not typically associated with a quantitative study.

Patton (2002) continued by describing qualitative research as "theory that emerges from the researcher's observations and interviews out in the real world" (p. 11).

The qualitative approach for this study required the distinct ability to explore experienced phenomena and perceptions of participants. Phenomenological research was designed to explore the structure and essence of the lived experiences of a group of people as related to a specific phenomenon (Patton, 2002). This phenomenological study aimed to explore the lived experiences of middle managers who managed an integration process during an M&A to fill a void in the literature.

Phenomenological studies typically used interviews to gather in-depth information about the participant and phenomena examined (McMillan & Schumacher, 2010). This phenomenological study used interviews to gather data as interviews were largely thought of in the literature as an effective means to capture comprehensive data. The aim of this phenomenological study was to explore participants' lived experiences with job-related, structural, and strategic uncertainty to further the understanding of this phenomenon. Patton (2002) suggested interviews were well-suited for unearthing new insights because they allowed for a highly detailed account from the participant perspective and provided opportunities to contrast the results with other experiences to create a better understanding about the phenomenon.

Population

A population was defined as "a group of elements of cases, whether individuals, objects, or events that conform to specific criteria and to which we intend to generalize the results of the research" (McMillian Schumacher, 2010, p. 129). The population for this study consisted of middle managers who worked in service-providing industries during an M&A integration process. Services-providing industries included educational and health services, trade, transportation, utilities, information, leisure and hospitality, consulting, and finance activities (Vollmer, 2016). The study focused on middle managers because of their role in leading employees and the literature suggested they had the influence needed to reduce uncertainty during an M&A process (Galpin & Herndon, 2014; Maepa, 2014). Middle managers were considered the organizational linchpins who guided the daily work duties and tasks of frontline employees as directed by top management (Ferry, 2010). The U.S. Department of Labor (2017a) reported 12,080,404 people were employed as middle managers, representing almost half (46.6%) of all management occupations (U. S. Department of Labor, 2017a).

 M&As in the United States flourished over the last few years. In 2014, 12,283 M&A transactions occurred valued at over 2.1 trillion dollars; in 2015, transactions increased to 12,885 totaling over 2.4 trillion dollars (Institute for Mergers, Acquisitions & Alliances [IMAA], 2018b). Transactions also increased in 2016 to 13,430; however, the value of M&A activity dropped to 1.7 trillion dollars (IMAA, 2018b). Southern California M&A transactions comprised 6.6% of all 2014 U.S. M&A deals, but in 2015 dropped to 5.8% and continued the trend in 2016 dropping to 5.1% (Claremont McKenna College, 2018; IMAA, 2018b). For this study, organizations that operated in southern California were selected as a key criterion for the population. This region was chosen for convenience purposes and because of ample access to companies engaged in an M&A deal.

In addition to being in southern California, organizations used in this study were in service-providing industries. At the end of 2015, the private sector had 127 million jobs split between goods-producing and service-producing companies (U.S. Department of Labor, 2018b). Goods-producing industries accounted for 21 million jobs whereas service-producing industries accounted for 106 million jobs (U.S. Department of Labor, 2018b). Of the 12 largest M&A deals in the first half of 2016, eight companies provided services whereas only four focused on product manufacturing and development (Shen, 2016). The industries that conducted the most deals and had the highest values included healthcare, energy and power, technology, finance, and media and entertainment (IMAA, 2018). Service-producing companies that operated in southern California region that recently underwent an M&A were utilized for this study.

Sample

A sample is "the group of subjects or participants from whom the data are collected" (McMillan & Schumacher, 2010, p. 129). Purposive sampling was utilized in this study to obtain an appropriate sample. Patten (2012) described purposive sampling as a process in which the researcher determined the research focus and identified specific participants within the population who could provide deep insights related to the focus area. Although purposive sampling has its share of critics,

Patton (2002) argued purposeful sampling remains a reliable form of sampling because it focuses on studying information-rich participants knowledgeable about the topic in question.

Critics argue purposive sampling opens a study up for researcher bias (McMillan & Schumacher, 2010). To control for researcher bias, appropriate selection criteria and vetting processes were utilized to ensure participants had firsthand experience with the phenomena studied and could provide information about the topic.

For this study, the researcher relied on six professionals located in southern California, all with M&A experience, to identify potential sample members. The recommended sample members were asked to confirm they met the criteria for this study before completing the informed consent form (Appendix C). Any candidates who did not meet the criteria during the vetting process were thanked for their interest and dismissed from the study. All candidates who fulfilled the criteria were moved forward as participants in the research.

Selection Criteria

To garner the strongest results possible and protect the validity of the study, the following selection criteria were established:

Middle Management – the participant needed to work in the capacity of a middle manager within the larger organization

Recent M&A Activity – the participant had to be employed by a company when it went through the M&A integration process with the M&A occurring within the past three years

Integration Involvement – the participant had to be responsible for tasks associated with the M&A integration process

Team Interaction – the participant managed a team of three or more people during the M&A integration process

Service-Producing Industry – the company undergoing the M&A integration process had to be service-producing

Southern California Region – the participant had to employed by a company with operations in southern California

McMillan and Schumacher (2010) proposed sample sizes for qualitative studies should be determined based on the study's purpose and focus, data collection methods, participant accessibility, and level of data redundancy. The overall goal was to include as many information-rich participants as necessary until reaching redundancy, or the inability to produce new information within the study (Lincoln & Guba, 1985). McMillan and Schumacher (2010) suggested an ideal number of respondents in a qualitative study was between 20 and 30, unless the data became redundant. In this research, 15 middle managers who met the study criteria served as research participants.

Instrumentation

Interviews can be conducted using standardized instruments, semi-structured instruments, or open dialogue. Standardized open-ended interviews allow participants to use their own words to describe their experience of a phenomenon while asking all participants the same questions in the same order (McMillan & Schumacher, 2010). The technique provides participants the opportunity to respond freely while maintaining a specific focus for each question (McMillan & Schumacher, 2010; Patton, 2002). Patton (2002) acknowledged a weakness of standardized open-ended interviews, noting the researcher was confined to the predetermined topic and had minimal flexibility for exploring contiguous concepts and ideas. McMillan and Schumacher (2010) cautioned utilizing standardized open-ended interview questions required thorough preparation as little deviation was allowed during the interview. Patton (2002) countered this contention and suggested a consistent interview approach enabled the researcher to provide each study participant with identical interview processes, which minimized bias. To control for researcher bias, interview questions were predetermined and asked in the same order, and additional probing questions were asked when additional clarification was needed.

McMillan and Schumacher's (2010) advice was heeded during the preparation of the study and an expert panel reviewed all interview protocols. This panel consisted of three experts who held doctoral degrees. Two members on the expert panel had direct experience undergoing an M&A integration processes, which made them subject matter experts. The third panel member was an experienced researcher who provided feedback on the instrument. These experts comprised the panel that provided feedback to the researcher regarding the instrument and its appropriateness for this study.

The interviews lasted an average of 38 minutes in length and consisted of 12 interview questions with probing follow-up questions when needed. The interview questions were based on the four research questions put through the lens of Bordia et al.'s (2004) uncertainty model that featured strategic, structural, and job-related uncertainties. This yielded 12 interview questions with two additional probing questions reserved for when clarification was needed. The interview questions were asked in a standardized order to reduce the potential for researcher bias and ensure a consistent interviewing method. The researcher used a predetermined script (Appendix A), which started by asking interviewees about their professional background. The purpose of asking about participant background was to allow the researcher to understand how participants viewed their role in the organization and to provide the researcher with context to effectively understand the responses.

Instrument Validity and Reliability

An instrument is only considered effective if it has both a high degree of validity and reliability. An instrument is considered valid when it "accurately performs the function(s) it is purported to perform" (Patten, 2012, p. 61). The open-ended interview format required careful understanding of the research's purpose to word questions that solicited appropriate responses. The researcher ensured the interview questions focused on the problem and did not explore different issues or concepts. After the expert panel reviewed the instrument, pilot testing was used to ensure validity. The instrument for this study underwent two pilot tests, one by two managers who experienced an M&A integration effort and the other by an independent research expert. All pilot testers experienced the interview process and provided feedback about the instrument, which highlighted any potential bias. The pilot testers assessed the questions for readability, relevance, and overall understanding, which ensured the instrument was able to obtain relevant information. Patten (2012) purported that experts could be especially effective as they refined interview questions and tested the validity of an instrument. Based on the feedback from the pilot test, revisions were made to the interview instrument until it was approved and finalized.

Reliability refers to an instrument's capacity for achieving consistent findings (Patten, 2012). Reliability within this study focused on producing an invariable interview process while limiting researcher bias to the greatest degree possible. Researcher bias can appear as wavering reassurance, changing in voice tonality, behaving differently with participants, and inconsistently supporting behaviors and responses (McMillan & Schumacher, 2010; Patton, 2002). Researcher bias was controlled by using a standardized interview protocol that was reviewed by and expert panel and pilot tested. Additionally, the interviewer was observed during the pilot test process to limit potential bias from questioning techniques, tone, and body language.

Data Collection

Data collected for this study was achieved through a standardized interview process. In preparation for data collection, all participants received a correspondence from the researcher detailing the purpose of the research, procedures that would be used, and their involvement in the data gathering process. The correspondence also asked each participant to self-certify he or she met the selection criteria. Once it was established the potential participant met the selection criteria, he or she was invited to be a part of the sample (Appendix B), asked to complete an informed consent document (Appendix C), and provided a detailed schedule of the study. All consent forms were signed and either scanned or faxed to the researcher before participants were admitted into the study. The informed consent included the purpose of the research, the information to be collected and used, a confidentiality clause, and information about the risks and advantages that could potentially come from the interview. The confidentiality clause explained participant names and responses would be numerically coded to ensure the highest standards of confidentiality. After participants completed the informed consent form, interviews were scheduled based on each individual's availability.

Patten (2012) proffered that interviews should be conducted face-to-face when possible, unless accessibility and scheduling were problematic. It was the goal of the researcher to secure as many face-to-face interactions as possible. However, scheduling limitations called for most interviews to be conducted via phone call. Of the 15 interviews, three were conducted in-person.

All interviews were conducted using the same set of open-ended questions (Appendix A). The only deviation from the questions consisted of using two standardized clarification questions as needed. This was done to allow for additional clarification without influencing answers through biased wording or questioning.

When conducting interviews, a researcher must capture extensive amounts of information. Multiple researchers suggested note-taking was a critical facet of an interview process and recommended interviews be recorded to allow the researcher to revisit the sessions to ensure comprehensive information was captured appropriately for each participant (McMillan & Schumacher, 2010; Patten, 2012; Patton, 2002). Consistent with these best practices, the researcher took detailed notes during the interview process and recorded the sessions, which were used for transcription purposes after the interviews occurred.

Upon completion of the interviews, a follow-up email was sent to thank each respondent for participating and offer a summative report after the study. Table 2 displays the sequence of correspondence and time frames in which communication occurred.

Table 2

Dates for Participant Communication and Interviews

Activity	Start Date	End Date
Introductory Phone Call/Email	06/01/2016	09/15/2016
Email with Informed Consent and Scheduling	06/01/2016	09/24/2016
Interviews Conducted	06/15/2016	09/24/2016
Thank You Follow Up Email Sent	06/16/2016	09/25/2016
Summation of Findings Email Sent	01/30/2019	02/28/2019

To ensure the richest data possible, interviews were electronically recorded and transcribed by the researcher to keep an accurate account of each participant's responses. To ensure confidentiality, all participant names and responses were numerically coded. The data and transcriptions were stored on a password-protected computer. Six months after the dissertation defense and final university processes were completed, all data were destroyed.

Data Analysis

Patton (2002) remarked, "How you study the world determines what you learn about the world" (p. 125), which was an important consideration when analyzing the data gathered in this study. To analyze the data, all recorded interviews were transcribed in Microsoft Word. Researcher notes were added to the end of each transcript for a complete summation of the interview. The data were then reviewed for themes and codes were assigned. Birks and Mills (2015) suggested theoretical coding as an analysis tool because it provides the opportunity to explore data and understand it in greater detail to help describe phenomena.

For this study, thematic coding was largely based on the literature review as it revealed potential themes already widely accepted. The transcripts were read through to reveal overarching patterns and unique characteristics about respondent answers. Although initial coding of themes was important, this analysis required the researcher to understand the meaning behind the experience of the participants and the greater population. Creating meaning from the data gathered required the assembly the various answers from interview questions to compose a holistic viewpoint of uncertainty from strategic, structural, and job-related levels amidst an M&A integration processes. The themes were then coordinated on a larger scale to understand the perspective of middle managers as they experienced this phenomenon.

Analysis of data could be highly subjective, which created the potential for researcher bias. Birks and Mills (2015) stated researchers should use all available resources and existing theories to support and reinforce any findings as data analysis occurred. Excel sheets and hand-written charts were used for the analysis of the interview data during initial coding. This approach allowed the researcher to perform two critical coding functions, one based on the number of times words and phrases appeared and the other based on thematic elements of the transcripts. Additionally, this approach enabled the researcher to unmask colloquial terms and metaphors commonly used by managers in describing their experiences. In both cases, the charts and graphs needed a thorough review by the researcher to ensure the coding terminology was consistent for all the data.

To further counter potential bias, the researcher secured an outside researcher to conduct an independent analysis. This outsider researcher was a professional experienced in research techniques and data analysis, and a subject matter expert. The researcher and outside researcher met and exchanged codes for the data to test for reliability of the results. The outside researcher coded 10% of the total data and compared it to the researcher's findings. Inter-rater reliability between coders must be above 80% to assume reliable findings, with above 90% preferred (Lombard, Snyder-Dutch, & Bracken, 2004). For this study, the outside researcher's agreement with the coding was 95%, which indicated reliable coding.

Analyzing data occurred in multiple rounds until the data were thoroughly vetted and connected to pertinent themes and codes. The analysis required the researcher to evaluate the themes multiple times as patterns and themes evolved throughout the analytical process. The rounds included trend analysis, data congruency, grouping of themes, establishing thresholds, and outside researcher corroboration. When the data analysis reached a point of redundant saturation, findings were determined because no new data would be revealed through further analysis. These data were then crafted into a synthesized document, which was used as a springboard establishing findings.

Limitations

This study recognized possible limitations of this research, which included:
1. This study consisted of a small sample, limiting the validity and generalizability the data
2. The use of structured interview questions could limit participant responses
3. This study focused on middle managers who may experience the M&A process differently than other levels of the company
4. This study was limited to southern California, so the result may not be generalized to other regions of the state or country

Summary

Chapter III outlined the design of the study, population, sample, instrumentation, data collection techniques, data analysis, and limitations. The population used for this study was middle managers who managed a team during an M&A process. These middle managers were selected based upon a set of criteria and were interviewed to record their perspectives and experiences regarding uncertainty during the M&A process. The study abided by the highest standards of research to protect participant confidentiality. The data collection and analysis aimed to build convergence and divergence from participant responses. Lastly, the limitations detailed aspects of the study that could present potential issues and challenges. Chapter IV presents the analysis of the data.

CHAPTER IV: RESEARCH, DATA COLLECTION, AND FINDINGS

Chapter IV reiterates the purpose of the study, research questions, population, and sample, and presents a thorough analysis of the findings for each research question. The results explore how participants perceived uncertainty was managed during the integration process. The results further report participants' views on the strategies perceived to be effective and ineffective and participant recommendations regarding strategies to manage uncertainty during an integration process.

Purpose Statement

The purpose of this qualitative study was to explore

middle managers' perceptions about how organizations manage job related, structural, and strategic uncertainty during a merger and acquisition (M&A) integration process. Further, this research investigated what strategies middle managers perceived effective and ineffective for managing job related, structural, and strategic uncertainty during an M&A integration process. Finally, this study worked to identify the strategies middle managers recommended to manage job related, structural, and strategic uncertainty during an M&A integration process.

Research Questions

The following research questions served as a basis for this study:

1. How did middle managers perceive organizations managed job-related, structural, and strategic uncertainty during an M&A integration process?

2. What strategies did middle managers perceive to be effective for managing job-related, structural, and strategic uncertainty during an M&A integration process?

3. What strategies did middle managers perceive to be effective for managing job-related, structural, and strategic uncertainty during an M&A integration process?

4. What recommendations did middle managers make for managing job-related, structural, and strategic uncertainty during an M&A integration process?

Research Methods and Data Collection Procedures

A qualitative approach was used for this research, specifically calling upon phenomenology as a design approach. Phenomenology is a research design effective for gathering data about the lived experiences of individuals or groups (Patton, 2002). All data were gathered from interviews, which averaged approximately 38 minutes in length, where middle managers were asked about their experiences during an integration process following an M&A. The interview questions focused on job-related, structural, and strategic uncertainty and strategies used and recommended during integration processes.

The interview process consisted of 12 questions. Interviews were audio recorded using a digital recording device. Recordings were transcribed and used to ensure the accuracy of the participants' statements and to create transcripts. The researcher followed a structured interview script, (Appendix A) that outlined the parameters of the research and provided a standard format for all participants. Participants were first asked to provide their background to the researcher for context regarding their role during the integration process, which also confirmed all selection criteria were fulfilled. The researcher followed the interview questions in order without deviation. At the end of the interviews, participants were asked if they wanted to share any additional thoughts, providing an opportunity to capture the richest data possible.

Population

The population for this study consisted of middle managers who worked in service-providing industries during an M&A integration process. Services-producing industries included educational and health services, trade, transportation, utilities, information, leisure and hospitality, consultation, and finance (Vollmer, 2016). In addition, participants had to meet five other criteria: worked as a middle manager, employed during an integration process within the last three years, involved in the integration process, managed a team of at least three staff, and worked for a company with operations in southern California. The study focused on middle managers because of their role in leading employees and the literature suggested they could reduce uncertainty during an M&A process.

Sample

The researcher utilized purposeful sampling to identify 10 qualified professionals across various industries to ensure the sample represented a variety of organizations in service-producing industries. A total of 32 potential participants were contacted for this research; however, seven were unable to be reached. The researcher provided 25 of the 32 (78%) potential respondents with the selection criteria. Ten of the potential participants did not meet the criteria and were rejected due to the time elapsed since their integration experience, their role in the company, or confidentiality issues that prevented them from disclosing their experiences. The remaining 15 respondents met the established criteria, consented to participate, and were interviewed. For this sample, 11 of the 15 participant's companies were acquired as opposed to four of the participants whose companies were acquiring other organizations.

Demographic Data

Demographic data were collected to identify the industries where the participants worked. The six industries represented in this study were consulting, finance, health services, information, trade, and transportation and utilities. Table 3 presents the industries, total participants in each industry, and the percentage of participants who identified that industry.

Table 3
Industry Breakdown of Study Participants

Industry	n	%
Consulting	2	13.3
Finance	4	26.7
Health Services	1	6.7
Information	2	13.3
Trade	4	26.7
Transportation and Utilities	2	13.3

Presentation and Analysis of Data

Data collected underwent a thorough coding and analysis process of theme exploration, identification, and analysis. Trend analysis uncovered themes based on the literature, meaning participant comments were analyzed and contrasted against the literature review. These themes were initially compared using a variety of post it charts and excel sheets. The next round of analysis involved two researchers reviewing the data to reduce bias and increase congruency between the data and themes as well as accuracy of the findings. These themes were then grouped into categories of job-related, structural, and strategic uncertainty, as well as combined uncertainty. The themes were reviewed again to ensure titles captured participant responses while conveying meaning for the integration. The final round of analysis involved determining appropriate thresholds for the research question. In total, six rounds of analysis were utilized along with two independent research experts.

Specific coding entailed a review of all transcripts and identification of major themes for each research question. Themes were referenced across all participants by research question. Research Question One focused on perceptions of uncertainty, whereas Two and Three focused on strategies used and Four focused on recommendations. Research Questions Two and Three had thresholds of 8/15 participants or at least 53%. For Research Question Four, two thresholds were utilized; the threshold for recommendations across all three types of uncertainty had was 8/15 (53%) and for individual types of uncertainty the threshold was 9/15 (60%).

For Research Question One, three main perceptions about how the integration was managed emerged. For Research Questions Two, Three, and Four, participants were asked to identify strategies and recommendations, many of which overlapped. Research Question Two had eight overall strategies identified as effective, with three specific to job-related uncertainty and five that applied to both structural uncertainty and strategic uncertainty. Research Question Three had six strategies perceived as ineffective, with four that cut across all three types of uncertainty, one specific to structural uncertainty, and one specific to strategic uncertainty. Research Question Four identified 202 recommendations to manage uncertainty during an integration process, with 11 recommendations relevant to all three types of uncertainty. Additionally, 14 recommendations were identified for job-related uncertainty, 15 for structural uncertainty, and 15 for strategic uncertainty. Table 4 presents the types of uncertainty and number of strategies or recommendations that hit the established threshold for Research Questions Two through Four.

Table 4

Number of Themes by Research Question and Type of Uncertainty

	Type of Uncertainty	# Strategies & Recommendations	Desired Threshold
Research Question 2	Job-Related	3	53%
	Structural	5	53%
	Strategic	5	53%
Research Question 3	Job-Related	4	53%
	Structural	5	53%
	Strategic	5	53%
Research Question 4	All Uncertainties	11	53%
	Job-Related	14	60%
	Structural	15	60%
	Strategic	15	60%

Note. Some strategies applied two or more types of uncertainty, but are represented under each applicable type within the table.

An independent research professional was utilized to increase the research validity by checking for bias and ensuring themes were accurately and consistently identified across all interview questions and types of uncertainty. This independent research professional earned a doctoral degree in organizational leadership, engages in professional research analysis daily, and has 20 years of specialized expertise within the research industry. This research professional analyzed each of the 12 interview questions based on coded data provided to confirm agreement of codes. The level of agreement between the researcher's analysis and the professional's analysis was 95%, which was above the 80% needed to ensure validity and reliability within a qualitative study (Lombard, Snyder-Duch, & Bracken, 2003).

Findings for Research Question One

Research Question One was: *How did middle managers perceive that organizations managed job-related, structural, and strategic uncertainty during an M&A integration process?*

Research Question One was asked three times to identify participant perceptions about how the organization managed job-related, structural, and strategic uncertainty during the integration process. Three codes were used to classify the perceptions of middle managers about the integration process, *Managed Well* (positive), *Parts Managed Well and Poorly* (mixed), and *Managed Poorly* (negative). As shown in Table 5, perceptions about job-related uncertainty were more mixed, perceptions of structural uncertainty were more negative, and perceptions of strategic uncertainty were more positive compared to the other two.

Table 5

Perceptions of How the Companies Managed Uncertainty by Type

	Job-Related		Structural		Strategic	
	n	%	n	%	n	%
Managed Well (Positive)	4	27	2	13	6	40
Mixed	5	33	4	27	6	40
Managed Poorly (Negative)	6	40	9	60	3	20

The following sections provide greater detail regarding

perceptions about how the different types of uncertainty were handled during the integration process after an M&A.

Perceptions of Managing Job-Related Uncertainty

The 27% of participants who perceived job-related uncertainty was managed well commented the acquiring company focused on providing clarity about the integration process and subsequent changes to help reduce job-related uncertainty. Those with mixed experiences indicated some aspects were managed well but other parts did not proceed as planned. Some explained the mixed perceptions were due to the need to balance information flow against the need to adhere to confidentiality agreements. Participant A013 illustrated this dynamic by sharing,

> It was difficult because... giving too much information and not giving enough information was a delicate balance. We wanted to be sure we gave them enough information so everyone wasn't stressed out, but not too much information so we weren't in breach with any of the contractual terms with the company that was acquiring us.

Six participants (40%) perceived job-related uncertainty was poorly managed during the integration process. The primary reason was lack of information given directly to employees. Often, employees received information through the rumor mill. Two participants described different experiences about how information was managed during the integration and how that impacted job-related uncertainty. Participant A003 explained, "We actually had heard of the merger coming before it was announced to us, somebody let it slip, which caused a lot of uncertainty right away." The information was not managed and thus increased job-related uncertainty. Participant A007 illustrated the congruence between communication and actions, saying, "Management...touted the mental health of the organization and that's hard to swallow when you repeatedly go through these organizational changes and watch people that have tenure with the company and were very good employees were no longer there." With job-related uncertainty, Participant A007 also shared management focused on certain aspects of the integration that did not translate into reducing job-related uncertainty for employees.

Perceptions of Managing Structural Uncertainty

Participants believed structural uncertainty during the integration process was poorly managed. Only two participants (13%) perceived the organization managed structural uncertainty well, four (27%) reported mixed perceptions, and nine (60%) noted the organization managed structural uncertainty poorly. One participant who noted structural uncertainty was well managed indicated the creation of a team to manage the integration process was effective. Participant A009 said,

> We will take some subject matter experts... from different areas and make them part of the integration process... We have a team that all they do is mergers and acquisitions from the financial and the bookkeeping... Then we always reach out to subject matter experts across the company to be part of that.

Participant A007 indicated structural uncertainty was not an issue, commenting "I don't know that I had a major problem with that... the organization was healthy and remained strong." In each of the cases where structural uncertainty was managed well, participants cited the organization had consistent intention about conducting the M&A.

Some of the circumstances that led to mixed perceptions included how systems were combined and failure to develop a plan to manage the integration process. Participant A002 remarked, "Merging those two cultures together as well as... the systems... is always a lengthy process... It just takes time and... to change and that's why it's important to be very careful about how you describe those changes." The time needed to nurture the integration process was often under-estimated by the acquiring company. Participant A015 elaborated to issues of timing, noting,

> Many times there is a quickness just to get the thing sold without necessarily the complete plan on transition. And those are one of the things that need to be really firmed up because it's very uncertain for the transition team and employees as it is, so they need something to grab onto to know what they can plan for.

Participants voiced several concerns regarding the lack of a full strategy for executing the integration process at the day-to-day level and how that impacted structural uncertainty. These concerns were reflected by 9 of 15 participants (60%) who noted most issues experienced stemmed from being unprepared for day-to-day operations during the integration process. Participant A011 characterized how their integration process functioned without a plan, stating, "There was no real strategy... to deal with structural uncertainty, it was just, at mid-level management there was no comment and you just observed it." Participant A003 had a similar experience of not being able to effectively maneuver integration duties, specifically around systems. Participant A003 shared "systems and reporting, that was a little difficult...because... we had the same software but... different information. When you tried to merge the two together it was difficult and there was not enough training on the differences of the new system." Both systems issues and lack of a clear plan to manage the integration process were consistently cited by participants.

Additional comments from nine participants noted structural uncertainty was poorly managed because the new organization's structure was not established. Participant A004 explained what happened when the newly formed organization was unable to provide specific details about structure. This participant perceived the lack of a clearly defined structure impacted the integration because,

> Day to day operations, systems... reporting structures... have not been clearly defined... that's probably one of the bigger challenges. The structure... had not been planned out prior to the announcement, so it is coming more on kind of a fly basis... which I think creates more uncertainty.

From a different perspective, Participant A005 explained how consistent change over time negatively impacted the organization, sharing,

> Unfortunately, our structural systems were in significant flux... and have been changing over the last

couple of years so we're in the middle of a pretty big structural change that hasn't...stabilized. I think you have a lot of demoralization... Just trying to learn all of this new stuff that's coming and now what's going to happen because of this acquisition...There has not been very much communication.

Participant A005 discussed how change became a major issue when it was left unmanaged and allowed to continue for long periods of time without a chance for the change to galvanize. Numerous factors contributed to 60% of participants citing structural uncertainty as poorly managed, including lack of an integration strategy, not defining the new organizational structure, and change without stabilization.

Perceptions of Managing Strategic Uncertainty

Perceptions regarding strategic uncertainty were more positive than perceptions about job-related and structural uncertainty. Six participants (40%) said the organization managed strategic uncertainty well, six (40%) said it was mixed, and only three (20%) said it was poorly managed.

Participants had a variety of examples to illustrate how strategic uncertainty was well managed. Participants noted the acquiring company clearly communicated the intentions behind the deal and had a defined plan that increased confidence in the health of the organization. Frequent and varied forms of communication paired with clearly defined plans resulted in more confidence in the organization. Participant A005 described how organization leadership was clear about their goals, saying they used "Lots of communication, ongoing communication for many years about our intention to do a merger or acquisition." Participant A011 further discussed the level of communication utilized about the strategic rationale throughout the integration process, stating "The communication was extremely good. It was pretty well understood why we were purchased and what the changes were in the market... it was clear from the beginning, from the executives down through to all levels of management."

In these integration examples, clear communication about the strategic rationale behind the integration was a key element. Participant A007 acknowledged the company "laid out what their plans were, it all looked rosy, and they followed through.... To grow the company, we... talked about that and being able to put those big names in their back pocket. It made the organization stronger." Six participants agreed when the organization communicated intentions clearly and worked to create a stronger organization, strategic uncertainty was well managed.

Most participants (60%) perceived that with strategic uncertainty, parts were managed well whereas other parts were managed poorly. For example, Participant A015 recounted an integration scenario where some of the plan was created but gaps remained over time, explaining,

> Everybody can see on a document who's in charge of what and what they're responsible for, their action items to get done... When the transition plan is done, where are we are going to want to be?...After that 90-day, after that year, then... what does this look like in a 5-year plan?

Similar to findings at the structural level, participants

stated a plan helped reduce strategic uncertainty about the longer-term vision and direction of the organization. A different integration situation spawned mixed results for Participant A004 with how strategic uncertainty was managed. Participant A004 outlined how integration was conducted at the strategic level, sharing,

> They let us know in a very clear way what their strengths were, why they were successful, what they're focused on, and what's important to them... it's been a very clear and concise consistent message of we do this, and we handle it this way, and this is why we're successful.

However, Participant A004 noted although this approach was not inherently detrimental, it neglected the operations and culture of the acquired company, which created strategic uncertainty. The mixed results managing strategic uncertainty came from having a partial plan but not integrating the culture and operations of the company in the integration process.

Only three (20%) participants indicated strategic uncertainty was poorly managed, commenting on negative impacts. Three participants cited disconnects in the decision-making processes as a factor that increased strategic uncertainty. Participant A003 noted strategic uncertainty was managed poorly because of disconnects between decision makers and decision implementers. Participant A003 shared, "It was not good at all... if the people knew at the high level what was going on in the weeds, like where we were at, they could have made better decisions." Additionally, Participant A001 noted the decision-making and rationale behind the acquisition was a primary concern, which increased strategic uncertainty, commenting,

I don't think they managed it very well... the reason they figured they should pursue another company is because there is something missing and... to fill something that's missing, they figure buying a company might be the quickest way to fill up that hole... In their minds, we could just buy a company that will give us a whole bunch of people and maybe even some projects and we'll hit the ground running and get to get started with a whole new focus on life.

Both integration situations detailed decisions made at the upper echelons of the organization, which created operational complexities and led to strategic uncertainty.

Findings for Research Question Two

Research Question Two was: *What strategies did middle managers perceive to be effective for managing job-related, structural, and strategic uncertainty during an M&A integration process?*

Research Question Two was asked three times to explore what strategies participants perceived to be effective to manage job-related, structural, and strategic uncertainty during the integration process. Across job-related, structural, and strategic uncertainty, 15 effective strategies were identified, with specific strategies that emerged as effective for each type of uncertainty. Within job-related uncertainty, three strategies were perceived to be effective by at least eight participants. For both structural and strategic uncertainty, the same five strategies were perceived as effective (Table 6).

Table 6

Effective Strategies for Managing Uncertainty During Integration

	Job-Related		Structural		Strategic	
	n	%	n	%	n	%
Communicating information to employees during the integration	11	73				
Using a variety of means and methods to deliver communication	11	73				
Employing frequent communication at the onset of the change	9	60				
Developing a strategy for achieving goals during integration			11	73	11	73
Creating an organizational structure with defined roles and responsibilities			10	67	11	73
Designing opportunities for staff to collaborate, cross pollinate, and learn from each other			9	60	9	60
Pulling best practices from both organizations			8	53	8	53
Focusing on the tasks, results, and employees during the process			8	53	8	53

The following sections provide additional description about the strategies perceived as effective for the different types of uncertainty. Given the similarity between structural and strategic uncertainty, these two areas are discussed together.

Effective Strategies for Managing Job-Related Uncertainty

Participants identified three specific strategies perceived as effective for managing job-related uncertainty, which all related to communication: communicating information to employees during the integration (n = 11, 73%), using a variety of means and methods to deliver communication (n = 11, 73%), and employing frequent communication at the onset of the change (n = 9, 60%).

The three strategies outlined different aspects of communication to help reduce job-related uncertainty during the integration process. Most participants agreed executives communicating information to employees and using a variety of methods to do so were both necessary for managing uncertainty. Participant A005 illustrated this point by sharing, "They communicated regularly...from the top down and ensured we communicated through our channels... There were emails, postings on a website, there were corporate videos from the top, there were virtual meetings, there were in-person meetings at various levels." Additionally, 60% of participants perceived frequent communication at the beginning of the integration process as an effective strategy for reducing job-related uncertainty. Participant A011 described how information "was communicated down to the area managers, sector managers, and division managers." Participant A011 elaborated that frequent communication eased job-related uncertainty because as the acquiring company communicated, employees viewed the transition into the new organizational structure as more manageable.

Effective Strategies for Managing Structural and Strategic Uncertainty

Participants identified the same five strategies perceived to be effective for managing structural and strategic uncertainty: developing a strategy for achieving goals during integration (n = 11, 73%); creating an organizational structure defining roles and responsibilities (n = 10, 67%) and (n = 11, 73%); designing opportunities for the staff to collaborate, cross pollinate, and learn from each other (n = 9, 60%); pulling best practices from both organizations (n = 8, 53%); and focusing on tasks, results, and employees (n = 8, 53%).

Participant A013 drilled down further into developing a strategy for achieving goals, explaining the strategy included information on the new organizational structure to provide clarity, sharing, "You knew what the new dynamic was from the org charts...who was going to do what." Similarly, Participant A004 described, "An effective strategy was being up front...and being clear about what they were trying to do and why they were doing it."

Defining clear roles and responsibilities was also effective in managing structural and strategic uncertainty, as indicated by 60% of participants. As Participant A013 remarked, structures regarding roles and responsibilities allowed integration to be effectively conducted. Additionally, Participant A009 highlighted the importance of ensuring the organizational structure was well defined, suggesting a company lay out "here's how we are going to change the operations, here's how we are going to change the organizational structure," and avoid surprises.

Creating opportunities for staff from both organizations to collaborate and learn from each other was also an effective strategy for managing uncertainty. Participant A003 illuminated this importance, saying, "You got to make time to meet with that other team over there because we want to roll out successfully and they want to roll in successfully." Participant A003 also recalled opportunities for staff to learn from one another, sharing, "They showed us how to accomplish things correctly in their system, and in turn we were able to help them read our system, which gave us, the staff, a sense of value still." This concept aligned with the next effective strategy, pulling best practices from both organizations. Participant A011 recounted time spent discussing best practices, saying, "The business development team spent an enormous amount of time communicating around the growth potential and the synergies between how teams would coordinate together." By focusing on both organizations, best practices could be adopted and allowed each company to bring their strengths to the newly combined entity. In contrast, half of participants (53%) noted uncertainty increased when the companies pulled most practices from only one of the companies as opposed to both, highlighting the need to merge best practices from both organizations to reduce strategic uncertainty.

The last strategy perceived as effective for managing structural uncertainty focused on balancing results, tasks, and employee needs. Participant A004 explained how the company focused on employees during the integration process, stating,

> There's been an allowance to ask questions about structural uncertainty, about the day to day operations, questions about the systems, questions about the reporting structure, and there's been multiple occasions where that's been available. And those lines of communications were wide open.

Making efforts to communicate with staff, develop strategies, define roles and responsibilities, provide opportunities for cross-team collaboration, integrate best practices from both organizations, and focus on the tasks and employees were effective strategies to mitigate uncertainty during an integration process.

Findings Related to Research Question Three

Research Question Three was: *What strategies did middle managers perceive to be ineffective for managing job-related, structural, and strategic uncertainty during an M&A integration process?*

Research Question Three was asked three times to explore participant perceptions about strategies perceived to be ineffective for managing job-related, structural, and strategic uncertainty. Across job-related, structural, and strategic uncertainty, six ineffective strategies were identified that met the threshold for inclusion in the study, and there was great overlap across the three types of uncertainty. Four strategies were common across all three types of uncertainty, with one strategy that applied solely to structural uncertainty and one that applied solely to strategic uncertainty (Table 7).

Table 7

Ineffective Strategies for Managing Uncertainty During Integration

	Job-Related		Structural		Strategic	
	n	%	n	%	n	%
Executives attempted to maintain latitude in communication and sharing information	13	87	12	80	11	73
Too much focus on transactional elem-	14	93	13	87	9	60

ents of the integration process						
Use of an incremental planning process	10	67	12	80	8	53
Use of a transactional approach to lead change and achieve results	9	60	10	67	8	53
Only top executives managed integration efforts			8	53		
Integration duties were added to existing workloads to minimize expenditures					8	53

Ineffective Strategies for Managing Uncertainty

Due to the high degree of overlap in strategies deemed ineffective for managing uncertainty, all three types of uncertainty are discussed in tandem. This is followed by a description of the two strategies that only applied to one type of uncertainty.

Executives attempted to maintain latitude in communication and sharing information. To maintain agility during changing conditions, executives attempted to maintain latitude in communication. This was often perceived as the withholding of information and was received poorly by the employees. Participant A011 detailed this dynamic and the unintended consequences saying, "I noticed some carefulness around the communication that it did not come in the form of memo and I imagine that's because… they didn't want it to be quoted or referenced again because things change." Participants agreed communication flow from executives was the most critical because it outlined the direction for the M&A for employees to be able to follow. However, Participant A003 described how the CEO tried to maintain latitude around the information shared, noting, "When we met with him... we thought, okay great, here's the top guy ready to answer our questions. He just kept saying, I can't say, I can't say." Without the necessary information, participants described difficulty functioning in their roles. Participants acknowledge the release of information needed to be carefully timed and understood the need to balance the release of information and need to maintain confidentiality agreements, but results indicated this approach yielded mixed results. Participants remarked it was difficult to manage day-to-day operations when the information needed to understand the new organizational structure was not communicated consistently or effectively. Participant A011 commented on the unintended consequences of the approach, "There was some purposeful lack of information around restructuring. And... that generally creates uncertainty."

Too much focus on transactional elements of the integration process. Two strategies identified as ineffective addressed a transactional approach to managing the integration processes. The first related to management taking a high task orientation during the integration process with a strong focus completing tasks and realizing the intended M&A results. Participant A004 emphasizes how a transactional approach can impact employees,

> There's a substantial amount of layoffs... and it was communicated very early, which I think was a mistake... communication is key, but to provide notification to individuals that they will no longer have a job... and to give no assurances that they'll have

something to go to next, then that in turn affects morale, it creates panic, and it creates... a lack of interest or investment in their job.

Participant A006 further underscored this concern,

We never acknowledged when a person left... we just learned to adapt and you would show up, somebody wouldn't be at a meeting and you'd wait until the second meeting, if he wasn't there... I'd evaluate what were his responsibilities that impacted me and let's divvy those up.

Participant A007 described an unintended consequence of a transactional approach guided how the company operated,

People were working long number of hours, many times over holidays, and I'm talking Christmas day to support the growth and these large clients.... programming had to be done to meet their expectations .... I was surprised that employees lasted as long as they did, for years even, under that kind of pressure.

This transactional approach created several concerns and issues for employees as they were implementing the integration activities on a day-to-day basis. Most participants commented that executives focusing on transactional parts of the integration was not effective for reducing uncertainty. Participant A006 discussed, "We never once heard from management. You would hear from just district managers and you would hear from territory managers, but you never heard from anybody at a vice president level or above." Participant A006 noted this approach was perceived as transactional because there were no interactions with the top leadership of the integrated organization. These transactional tactics hindered integration efforts by not considering the employee role within integration implementation at the structural level. Participants viewed executives who utilized a transactional leadership approach as ineffective in reducing uncertainty.

Use of an incremental planning process. An incremental planning process during integration was also perceived as ineffective to reduce uncertainty and participants identified this as a challenge. Participants perceived the acquiring companies lacked a solid plan for the integration, resulting in impromptu decision-making and limited predictability. Participant A010 described how incremental planning efforts impacted employees, sharing, "They didn't seem to plan out how quickly the changes can be integrated in the merging of organizations... they set this quick process to flow together and it hasn't flowed smoothly."

Participant A013 described an experience believed to be common in many integrations, "We did not have a formal strategy...It was very informal, there was just a couple of us handling everything ad hoc for the entire merger and acquisition... and dispersing the information accordingly and making changes accordingly." Participant A004 further illustrated an issue with the incremental planning process during integration, stating, "You can ask the question as much as you want, but if there's no plan in place, you get the same answer...in a merger acquisition scenario you should already, for the most part, have your plan set in place." The incremental planning process did not support predictability or provide clarity about the organizational structure, thus increasing uncertainty.

Use of a transactional approach to lead change and achieve results. Participants agreed a company focused solely on transactional aspects of integration to achieve results without consideration for employees was ineffective in reducing uncertainty. A transactional approach focused on tasks and results as opposed to employees, an approach largely considered ineffective for reducing all three types of uncertainty.

Other ineffective strategies for managing uncertainty. Two additional strategies met the minimum threshold to be a key finding. One related to structural uncertainty and the other to strategic uncertainty.

An ineffective strategy specific to structural uncertainty was relying solely on executives to manage integration efforts form the top level of the organization. Participant A003 explained executives started to make changes without fully understanding how it would impact operations, stating, "They started not allowing us to participate in the month end process… We found out afterwards that things didn't go well, but had we been involved it probably would have gone better." Participants noted the organizational knowledge held by employees was critical for executing the integration process, but this knowledge was underutilized by executives.

Half of participants (53%) purported that when companies added integration-related duties or duties held previously by team members who did not remain with the organization to existing workloads, strategic uncertainty was impacted. One scenario described by Participant A012 emphasized how laying off employees and shifting responsibilities without a plan impacted the integration, sharing,

> They were laying off people left and right that had key roles. And they were laying them off before they even really knew what was going on, so there was a

lot of stuff that happened after that employee was gone and... they didn't know how to fix things.

At the strategic level, executives were reducing the workforce without first understanding how those employees contributed to organizational operations. By removing employees without consideration for the integration, the remaining staff inherited duties to manage in addition to integration efforts and their normal work roles. In addition to an increase in stress, this also increased uncertainty.

Findings Related to Research Question Four

Research Question Four was: *What recommendations did middle managers make for managing job-related, structural, and strategic uncertainty during an M&A integration process?*

Research Question Four was asked three times to explore what recommendations participants made for managing job-related, structural, and strategic uncertainty during an M&A integration process. Across all three types of uncertainty, participants identified 202 recommendations, many of which overlapped between job-related, structural, and strategic uncertainty. From the 202 recommendations, 11 were common across all three types of uncertainty and met the threshold for study inclusion (Table 8). Within job-related uncertainty an additional 14 recommendations met the threshold, with another 15 for structural uncertainty and 15 for strategic uncertainty.

Table 8

Recommendations for Managing Uncertainty

	Type of Uncertainty	n	%
Communicate at every level of the organization	Job-Related	13	87
	Structural	11	73
	Strategic	13	87
Communicate without sharing privileged information	Job-Related	11	73
	Structural	11	73
	Strategic	14	93
Have consistent communication	Job-Related	11	73
	Structural	10	67
	Strategic	13	87
Answer employee questions	Job-Related	11	73
	Structural	10	67
	Strategic	13	87
Combine components of both cultures	Job-Related	10	67
	Structural	8	53
	Strategic	8	53
Have a detailed plan	Job-Related	8	53
	Structural	12	80
	Strategic	12	80
Have clear goals	Job-Related	8	53
	Structural	13	87
	Strategic	11	73
Have teams from both organizations working together	Job-Related	12	80
	Structural	9	60
	Strategic	12	80
Trust management	Job-Related	14	93
	Structural	8	53
	Strategic	13	87
Value employee knowledge, expertise, skills, and experience	Job-Related	11	73
	Structural	11	73
	Strategic	10	67
Value and respecting employees	Job-Related	13	87

Structural	12	80
Strategic	12	80

Participants identified a variety of recommendations for managing job-related, structural, and strategic uncertainty, which focused on core themes of communication, planning, team interaction, and valuing employees.

Recommendations Across all Types of Uncertainty

Themes related to communication. Participants identified communication as a key theme for reducing all three types of uncertainty. Within the theme of communication five recommendations from participants emerged: communicating at every level of the organization, communicating without sharing confidential information, having consistent communication, information sharing with employees, and answering employee questions. Participant A005 stated "Communication is huge when you're facing change" and participants believed communication at every level of the organization helped solve problems that arose. Numerous participants also commented that while communication was strong at the onset of the integration process, over time communication became inconsistent and less frequent. Participant A008 shared the need for "continued consistency in communication," which was recommended to manage all three types of uncertainty.

Participants acknowledged the need to keep certain information confidential, in accordance with confidentiality agreements, during the integration process, knowing employees should be informed regarding items that would impact their day-to-day roles without divulging confidential information. Perceptions about the importance of getting relevant details about the integration was noted by multiple participants, including Participant 003 who recommended managers ensure employee questions are answered. Participant A003 specifically stated, "Any questions should be answered. I don't think you should be afraid to ask a question." Participants remarked that when questioned were answered, employees were better able to function in their roles and more thoroughly support the integration process.

Themes related to planning. Participants identified the need for a strong plan, with clear goals, actions, and roles, to manage all three types of uncertainty. Problems occur without a detailed plan, as Participant A011 explained, "The plan was very top level and it got developed as it went, which probably created some issues." Numerous participants reinforced the need for a comprehensive and detailed plan as they perceived this level of a plan provided employees with the peace of mind needed to effectively function in their day-to-day roles. Participants also recommended that a detailed plan include clear goals for both the integration process and the organization. Participants asserted having clear goals gave employees direction and a basic plan of action to achieve the desired results for the integration process during a time when they are eager to prove themselves. Participant A006 described how goals were crafted during the integration process, sharing, "I'm a big fan of working backwards, what is the end goal that we're looking for… how do we achieve that, you work that back." Participants recommended a detailed plan, paired with clear goals, helped reduce all three types of uncertainty.

Themes related to team interactions. Numerous participants recommended when organizations merge, the acquiring company must focus on combining elements of both companies' cultures. Participant A008 illustrated what happened when there was minimal effort to preserve components of both cultures, sharing, "They really didn't take the time to understand how we did business, how we operated, what some of our... sacred cows were in terms of things that... we really thought would engage or disengage people if they were changed." Participants recommended putting efforts forward to combine elements of both cultures was important to managing all three types of uncertainty.

Themes related to valuing employees. The last recommendations identified by participants across all areas of uncertainty centered on valuing employees. Participants recommended the team managing the integration process needed to ensure they were valuing employee knowledge, expertise, skills, and experience. Numerous participants recommended finding ways to engage the strengths of the acquired employees within the new organization. Participant A004 described how this could look during an integration process, saying, "I want to find who the key players are in that organization I'm acquiring and put them in lead roles to then drive in effect a trickle-down effect to my organization." Many participants felt employees were the most essential piece of the organization because of their understanding of both the organization and its operations.

On a related note, participants recommended treating employees as people instead of a number in a transaction. Nearly all participants identified the need for employees to feel valued and respected. Participant A003 underscored these sentiments, saying, "It's real important for the staff members to still feel valuable." Valuing and respecting employees had a significant impact on engagement and performance as Participant A006 explained, "It was the small meetings with senior management and that caring touch. You felt like your voice mattered and because your voice mattered, you worked just as hard if not harder."

In addition to the recommended strategies relevant for all three types of uncertainty, other recommendations relevant to one or two types of uncertainty also emerged. The following sections describe additional recommendations that were mentioned by a minimum of 9/15 participants. It begins with job-related uncertainty, followed by structural and strategic. In cases where a recommendation applied to two types of uncertainty, the recommendation is presented where it first appears with a notation of which additional type of uncertainty the recommendation applied.

Recommendations for Managing Job-Related Uncertainty

A common recommendation for reducing job-related uncertainty was utilizing leadership and management practices to conduct integration (which was also mentioned for managing structural uncertainty). Most participants (87%) identified this as critical in managing job-related and structural uncertainty. Some effective leadership practices recommended included honesty, transparency, cultural assimilation, and respect for employees during integration. Multiple participants commented on the need for honesty from management during the integration process to help reduce job-related uncertainty. Participant A014 described how use of certain language reduced trust and increased job-related uncertainty, explaining,

> I would have been completely honest in terms of any changes that were going to take place. They assured everybody up front that there were going to be no changes and that's just not a reasonable statement... when you have a company that's taking over another company.

Similarly, Participant A015 highlighted the need for transparency during the integration, stating,

> I'm all about transparency, let's all know who's in the game, who's got the power, where do we go, how's it going to affect the other department, you're kind of almost setting the vision... So, if you want employees to buy into your game, buy into your business, buy into your goals, to make whatever you want to make for the company, transparency is real important.

Additionally, participants included considering the newly acquired company's culture when planning integration efforts and respect for employees as effective leadership practices during an M&A process. Two thirds of participants (67%) recommended management understand cultural differences and similarities to allow the integration process to be navigated more successfully. Participant A008 stated, "having a really solid knowledge of the group coming in would have been imperative, going through the integration process." Numerous participants commented that not understanding differences and similarities often led to issues and problems that could have been avoided. In addition to respecting organizational cultures, many participants (73%) remarked the acquiring company should ensure the business deal is conducted with respect for employees and the uncertainty they feel about the longevity of their jobs. Participant A015 elaborated,

> They need to pour some confidence into those employees so that they know, they're livelihood is not necessarily going to be taken away or if it is then what the next steps are… it's a tough line to balance because… all the information that goes on is crazy.

Participants provided several specific recommendations related to managing job-related uncertainty for employees, which included reducing stress, anxiety, and surprises, and increasing engagement. Participants recommended the organization find productive methods or processes to help reduce employee stress during integration, asserting that by communicating information that matters to employees, anxiety could be reduced. Participant A008 illustrated this when saying, "in a period of uncertainty, people really want to know at the end of the day what's in it for them and how it's going to change their job."

Another theme that emerged was fostering opportunities for executives, middle managers, and employees to interact in-person or virtually. These interactions could come in a variety of forms as Participant A011 described,

> Executive level communication is important… having a portal or a website or some sort of social media ability to interact regarding the integration is really helpful, so some sort of status… where are we so people can understand what…is happening next

month or this portion of the activity.

Participants also discussed how an organization should focus on limiting surprises by sharing appropriate information with employees. Participant A013 recommended the organization provide "[employees] all of the information possible up front...so they don't get stressed out and they know at the end of the day what it's going to look like as much as possible." Limiting surprises through communication also could increase engagement, which Participant A013 noted, "buy-in is huge... getting everybody on board and that this is going to be for the best." Participants commented engaging employees in the integration process was vital and resulted in more support of the integration process and reduced job-related uncertainty.

Recommendations for Managing Structural Uncertainty

Participants identified a variety of recommendations for managing structural uncertainty. Many participants described how intentional planning enabled middle managers to implement the integration process effectively, which helped reduce structural uncertainty. Participant A004 highlighted the importance of intentional planning, noting the need for "a clear concise plan for execution because regardless of the fact if it's good or bad news, people are going to be more accepting if they have a clear understanding of why things are happening and how they're being administered." Numerous participants purported that if employees were overlooked during the planning process for the integration, disconnects between decision-making and execution resulted. Participants believed intentional planning empowered middle managers to assist in both the planning and execution of the integration tasks.

Another theme that emerged was the need for executives to understand employee roles before making decisions that impact daily operations. Participants were insistent that when executives understood employee day-to-day work, they were better equipped to make decisions and avoid creating adverse effects on the integration process. Participant A001 illustrated how decision-making trickles down, commenting,

> At the CEO and COO level... they need to involve a lot more of the workers to understand if it's a good idea to do this or not because ultimately, when they have acquired the company and they have signed all of the paperwork, they then drop it in the laps of the workers and say, "okay make it work" and they can't make it work if they weren't a part of the process to begin with.

Many participants recommended treating the integration like a project and using effective project management strategies such as communicating employee roles and engaging staff in decision-making process. This included valuing employees, as Participant A012 explained, "They should definitely try to help the employees as much as possible instead of treating them like a number." Participant A004 described the need for "understanding of capacities of people up front and how to put the right people in the right place and shuffle, allowing to shuffle as opposed to just making cuts right off the bat." A number of participants also believed executives should seek input to inform decision-making because the employees were ultimately executing those decisions during the integration process.

Participants recommended the acquiring organization should evaluate methods to improve systems, eliminate redundancies, and maximize efficiencies. Numerous participants discussed how having employees work with obsolete systems was detrimental to performance and productivity. Furthermore, participants understood updating systems was not always ideal given resource and financial constraints, but could be strategic during the integration process as staff were already adapting to major changes. Multiple participants asserted the integration process provided a valuable time to update operating systems as long as changes were clearly communicated to employees.

Another theme that emerged from the recommendations for managing structural uncertainty was mitigating potential conflicts of interests and increasing organizational value. Participants described the mitigation of conflicts of interest as ensuring the two companies did not pose risks to one another. Participant A001 recommended, "Before they do the acquisition, the acquiring company needs to ask themselves are there any projects at risk if we purchase this company." Numerous participants agreed with this sentiment, saying it was necessary to examine possible conflicts when considering the potential acquisition.

Participants also discussed the need for a compelling vision so executives can provide clear direction for team members. Participant A011 shared, "I think it's really important to explain to all levels and all staff why the purchase is good for the purchasing company and why the purchase is good for the company that was bought." A common understanding about the goals, intended outcomes, and reasons behind the M&A can help all staff work toward that shared vision.

Recommendations for Managing Strategic Uncertainty

Participants identified a variety of recommendations for managing strategic uncertainty during the integration process. A set of recommendations to manage strategic uncertainty related to communication, which included executives engaging in constructive communication with employees and frequent communication through a variety of mediums. Many participants recommended executives use constructive communication with employees; Participant A008 explained, "Having an opportunity for employees to speak with leaders in person... people will look to their leadership for their take on the direction and certainty or uncertainty." This communication could and should be delivered through several different channels. Participants recommended the acquiring company should utilize emails, webinars, calls, roadshows, websites or portals, videos, and in-person meetings to share information and gain input.

Participants recommended honesty and transparency as important for managing strategic uncertainty during integration. Participant A002 believed "emphasizing rapport, trust, and honesty usually trumps any sort of problems or negative actions in situations." Participants stated that throughout the integration process, the level of trust between management and employees was dictated by the honesty from management. Additionally, many participants confirmed transparency from management and in-person interactions were needed for managing strategic uncertainty. Participant A013 explained, "the best way is always face-to-face since this is a scary time for everyone but if that's not possible, some sort of a weekly update, newsletter, or something like that." Participants also recommended opportunities for all executives, middle managers, and employees to interact in-person. Participant A004 noted the need for executive face-to-face interaction by saying "one-on-one interaction as much as possible from senior management is key."

Another recommendation for managing strategic uncertainty was to provide direction for the integration process, which included sharing a vision and defining roles and responsibilities. Over half of participants noted a shared vision was essential to reduce strategic uncertainty because it provided an overarching direction during integration. Participants recommended the vision espouse the future of the company and provide direction to help crystallize integration goals and objectives. Numerous participants recommended the acquiring company establish clear roles and responsibilities enabling employees to properly function in their positions. Participant A008 illustrated what happened without clear roles and responsibilities, saying "We've had a team, one team in particular that... has gotten shuffled around four or five times in the last three years under different leadership because the organization keeps changing the leadership structure of this one group." The constant reorganization of the team created high levels of uncertainty, whereas clear roles and responsibilities could have reduced uncertainty.

Another recommendation was to focus on short-term integration implementation to manage strategic uncertainty. Participant A006 explained short-term integration implementation, sharing, "It's bite sized goals that address the entire company in need. We got it for every area that the company does but they're easy, they're digestible, they're manageable." Numerous participants referenced the need for goals to be broken into smaller tasks for employees to focus on and complete.

Another key theme that emerged was the need to focus on the human element of the integration. Specific recommendations included respecting employees and limiting surprises. Participants recognized M&As as business deals, but still commented they should be conducted with respect for employees. Participant A013 recommended the need to humanize the transaction, noting it is "extremely important to remember, that while it is a business transaction... these are people who are feeding their families and providing insurance for their families." Participants also recommended a focus on reducing surprises. Over half of participants expressed the need to limit surprises to keep uncertainty manageable through the integration. Participant A002 recommended one approach for curbing surprises, saying, "You just want to be as straight forward as possible within appropriate time frames." Participants believed fewer surprises reduced uncertainty because employees knew what to expect. Keeping a focus on the human element of integration also offered reassurance to the staff, thus reducing uncertainty.

Summary

Chapter IV presented the data collected throughout the research study regarding perceptions, strategies, and recommendations for managing job-related, structural, and strategic uncertainty during integration. Several themes emerged from the interviews and subsequent analysis that underwent multiple rounds of coding and synthesis. Key findings for this research study were summarized. Findings about middle manager perceptions of the integration process were mixed, with 27% indicating it was well managed, 33% indicating some aspects were down well and others poorly, and 40% indicating the integration was poorly managed.

When disaggregated by job-related, structural, and strategic uncertainty, similar patterns emerged. Participants also identified a multitude of strategies they perceived as effective and ineffective more managing the different types of uncertainty, with a high level of overlap in strategies for structural and strategic uncertainty. Additionally, participants offered numerous recommendations companies could use to decrease job-related, structural, and strategic uncertainty during an integration process after an M&A.

Chapter IV presented the findings from this study. Chapter V explores the results and conclusions generated from the study findings. It also presents implications for action, recommendations for future research, and concluding remarks from the researcher.

CHAPTER V: FINDINGS, CONCLUSIONS, & RECOMMENDATIONS

Chapter V provides an overview of the purpose of the study, research questions, sample, and methods used for the research. Additionally, this chapter outlines specific findings and conclusions drawn from the data. The last part of the chapter highlights the implications for action and recommendations for future research.

Review of the Problem

Mergers and acquisitions (M&As) increased in frequency over the last few decades as globalization forced businesses to seek alternative means of growth (Daly et al., 2004; IMAA, 2018a). This surge in M&As was accompanied by trillions of dollars funneled into this business activity over the past few years (Kim & Roumeliotis, 2014; KPMG, 2014). Deloitte (2015) analyzed M&A trends in their 2015 quarterly report, which indicated M&A activity in increased by nearly 25% over 2014 numbers. The amount of capital invested into M&As suggested these transactions became increasingly important in the business community; however, despite these increases, research showed M&As failed at alarming rates (Dunbar, 2013; Waldman & Javidan, 2009).

Although the research on failure rates varied, estimates indicated over 65% of M&As failed to achieve their goals, which resulted in huge financial and productivity losses (DePamphilis, 2009; Doseck, 2012; Marks & Mirvis, 2011). Harding and Rouse (2007) further suggested 53% of firms experienced a decrease in overall company value because of an M&A. Some authors argued the greatest probability for failure of M&As occurred during the integration process (Appelbaum et al., 2007; Weber & Drori, 2011). This was especially problematic as established M&A goals often relied heavily upon the integration process as the organizations aimed to consolidate operations, reduce redundancy, capitalize on synergies, expand market share, and ultimately increase value (Venema, 2015). Despite the importance of integration processes, they were often inadequately executed, resulting from disconnects between executives driving the overall business strategy and middle managers and frontline employees who most frequently execute the tasks needed to integrate the two firms (Björkman et al., 2007; Lakshman, 2011; Zollo & Singh, 2004). These matters were further complicated by the high levels of uncertainty that naturally occurred with a change of this magnitude.

Research was clear that high levels of uncertainty negatively impacted organizational effectiveness and productivity (PricewaterhouseCoopers [PwC], 2011). As such, integration processes could be undermined by employees until a better understanding of uncertainty emerges (Guindon, 2013; Mann, 2011). Both Waldman and Javidan (2009) and Weber and Drori (2011) suggested more comprehensive data were needed to understand how to effectively manage M&A integration processes. Simply stated, with over 65% of companies failing to properly integrate and realize preset expectations, new understandings need to pave the way for more sound and predictable business activity (Doseck, 2012; Marks & Mirvis, 2011).

Purpose Statement

The purpose of this qualitative study was to explore middle managers' perceptions about how organizations manage job related, structural, and strategic uncertainty during an M&A integration process. Further, this research investigated what strategies middle managers perceived effective and ineffective for managing job related, structural, and strategic uncertainty during an M&A integration process. Finally, this study worked to identify the strategies middle managers recommended to manage job related, structural, and strategic uncertainty during an M&A integration process.

Research Questions

The following research questions served as a basis for this study:

1. How did middle managers perceive organizations managed job-related, structural, and strategic uncertainty during an M&A integration process?

2. What strategies did middle managers perceive to be

effective for managing job-related, structural, and strategic uncertainty during an M&A integration process?

3. What strategies did middle managers perceive to be effective for managing job-related, structural, and strategic uncertainty during an M&A integration process?

4. What recommendations did middle managers make for managing job-related, structural, and strategic uncertainty during an M&A integration process?

Research Methods and Data Collection Procedures

This study employed a phenomenological methodology, which utilized interviews for data collection. To study perceptions about the integration process, this methodology allowed participants to explain their experiences in detail. Data were gathered through in-person and telephone interviews that lasted approximately 38 minutes each. The researcher utilized a standardized interview script and participants answered 14 questions about the integration process. The questions focused on perceptions of middle managers regarding the integration processes, effective and ineffective strategies, and recommendations to manage job-related, structural, and strategic uncertainty during an M&A integration process.

Collected data underwent a thorough coding process of theme identification, exploration, and analysis. Trends were analyzed and contrasted against the literature. Data analysis involved two researchers reviewing the data to reduce bias and to ensure congruency between the data and themes, with the aim of producing accurate findings. Once themes were identified, they were grouped into categories of job-related, structural, and strategic uncertainty, as well as combined uncertainty (meaning the theme crossed multiple types of uncertainty). The themes were reviewed again to ensure the titles appropriately captured participant responses while conveying meaning for those not intimately involved with the data collection. The final round of analysis involved establishing the appropriate thresholds to determine consistency across each research question. As a result of this analysis, the researcher determined data from Research Questions Two and Three would be reported when a threshold of 8/15 participants or at least 53% was achieved. For Research Question Four, which explored participant recommendations to reduce uncertainty, the researcher determined data would be reported when the recommendation crossed all three types of uncertainty and a threshold of 8/15 (53%) was achieved. For individual types of uncertainty, the researcher determined data would be reported when a threshold of 9/15 (60%) was achieved. In total, six rounds of analysis were utilized along with two independent research experts validating the researcher's decisions.

    The study population was derived from participants who met six criteria, which included being a middle manager, managing a team, and being directly involved in an integration within the last three years. These middle managers came from the following industries: consulting (13.3%), finance (26.7%), health services (6.7%), information (13.3%), trade (26.7%), and transportation and utilities (13.3%). Purposeful and snowball sampling yielded the sample population, which was comprised of 15 middle managers.

Major Findings

Research Question One

Research Question One explored how middle managers perceived their organizations managed job-related, structural, and strategic uncertainty during an M&A integration process.

Three codes were used to classify the perceptions, *Managed Well* (positive), *Parts Managed Well and Poorly* (mixed), and *Managed Poorly* (negative). Perceptions about job-related uncertainty were more mixed, perceptions of structural uncertainty were more negative, and perceptions of strategic uncertainty were more positive compared to the other two types of uncertainty.

Research Question Two

Research Question Two explored the strategies middle managers perceived to be effective for managing job-related, structural, and strategic uncertainty during an M&A integration process. Across all three types of uncertainty, 15 effective strategies were identified.

Within job-related uncertainty, three strategies were perceived to be effective that met the threshold for inclusion of this study; all three related to communication. Within structural and strategic uncertainty, the same five strategies were perceived to be effective: developing a strategy, defining roles and responsibilities, creating opportunities for collaboration, pulling best practices from both organizations, and focusing on the tasks, results, and employees during the process.

Research Question Three

Research Question Three explored the strategies middle managers perceived to be ineffective for managing job-related, structural, and strategic uncertainty during an M&A integration process. Across all three types of uncertainty, six ineffective strategies were identified that met the threshold for inclusion in the study, and there was great overlap across the three types of uncertainty. Four strategies appeared across all three types of uncertainty: executives maintaining latitude in communicating and sharing information, too much focus on transactional elements, use of an incremental planning process, and use of a transactional leadership approach. Only top executives managing integration efforts was an ineffective approach that applied solely to structural uncertainty and integration duties added to existing workloads to minimize expenditures applied solely to strategic uncertainty.

Research Question Four

Research Question Four explored recommendations participants made for managing job-related, structural, and strategic uncertainty during and M&A integration process. Across all three types of uncertainty, participants identified 202 recommendations, many of which overlapped between job-related, structural, and strategic uncertainty. From the 202 recommendations, 11 were common across all three types of uncertainty. These 11 recommendations were grouped into four themes: communication, planning, fostering opportunities for team interactions, and valuing employees. Other recommendations related to one to two types of uncertainty, but not all three.

Unexpected Findings

Two unexpected findings emerged from this research. The first unexpected finding was how eager participants were to integrate with the new company and their commitment to working with team members from the new organization toward common goals. Although one would expect resistance to integrating the two companies, as the literature suggested resistance to change was natural, this was not the participants' perceptions. When the integration process occurred, participants wanted opportunities for staff from the two organizations to meet, interact, and work with one another as opposed to operating separately in silos. Members from both organizations were eager to collaborate, establish new relationships, and offer resources and support.

The second unexpected finding was many of the items deemed ineffective linked to planning processes that were not comprehensive, were perceived as incremental in nature, and were poorly constructed. Participants perceived that over time, these incremental approaches weighed on employees and often resulted in change fatigue. The respondents did not believe resistance to the M&A was strong initially, but instead uncertainty and discontent rose when employees felt they were not provided the full picture or given opportunities to participate and offer value during the integration process. Although these planning components are basic management practices, they did not appear as strong pillars of integration efforts. More specifically, employees wanted more structure brought to the integration process through a clearly laid out plan, stronger communication, and more clearly defined roles.

Conclusions

This study sought to identify middle manager perceptions about how organizations managed job-related, structural, and strategic uncertainty during an M&A process. The study further examined the strategies middle managers perceived to be effective and ineffective for managing the three types of uncertainty and explored recommended strategies for managing uncertainty during an M&A integration process. The following conclusions were drawn from the findings.

1. If an organization were to focus on one area to improve results during the integration process, that focus should be on reducing structural uncertainty as this was the area identified by the middle managers as the largest opportunity for improvement. Investments in clearly defined structures and roles, and more intentional planning processes will increase productivity and have the largest positive impact on employee emotional well-being.

2. When planning the phases of an integration process, careful consideration must be given to the capacity of employees to manage change. Many challenges and recommendations identified in this study directly link to change management expertise. Organizations should employ and empower personnel with change management expertise to prepare for and lead integration processes. Acquiring companies would be well-served to build change management capacity in their organizations. Change management models that include a heavy emphasis on culture, employee mindset, and intentional communication should be selected to guide integration processes.

3. Educational institutions need to reexamine their curriculum in critical programs, such as the master's in business administration, to achieve a strong emphasis on effectively managing the integration process. To meet industry needs, educational programs should further update their curriculum to ensure graduates are prepared to lead wide-scale change.

4. Professional organizations should build service offerings for M&A. The business community must prioritize building capacity of firms and individuals to more effectively plan and manage M&As, with special attention given to the integration process.

5. Companies appear to be conducting thorough analysis and have a strong vetting process for the due diligence phase of the M&A, and their efforts to communicate the strategic rationale of the M&A were effective. However, the due diligence process fails to consider key components essential for the integration process. Adding in an analysis of systems, best practices, and culture, and developing an integration and communication plan during the due diligence process, would yield stronger operational results. After the deal is signed and the integration begins, the same level of thoroughness should be applied to planning and execution of the integration to ensure optimal outcomes.

6. There is a cost to poorly conducting integration processes. The financial risks are high and failure is costly in terms of profit and loss and productivity and turnover. By investing in some of the strategies recommended from this research, organizations can actively work to limit their financial risk and maximize returns.

7. A dedicated integration team should be appointed to develop a comprehensive integration plan, implement the plan, and monitor the integration process to ensure appropriate course corrections. This team should be created at the beginning of the integration process and be comprised of both domain and change management experts, while also ensuring the team has representation from both organizations involved in the M&A. This team should drive the integration process, paying particular attention to strategic planning, communication, and the needs of employees. Stark consideration should be given to the relative cost of hiring or staffing an integration team against the potential for lost value due to heightened uncertainty, lost productivity, lost key personnel, and integration failures. The integration team must be given the authority to make decisions and the support needed to implement those decisions, or the team will be unable to effectively deliver results.

8. Employees inherently need to feel valued and respected, and they want to contribute to organizational goals. When employees are respected and engaged, productivity remains high, employees are more open to the integration changes, and employees are committed to achieving results, even during times of harsh deadlines and heightened uncertainty. Both middle managers and executives must change their mindsets and step out of a task mode to approach operations from an employee development standpoint. Executives need to establish the direction for the M&A early, while also engaging and relying on team members with operational expertise. Executives should focus on setting an inclusive tone and ensuring impacts to employees are carefully considered at every stage of the integration process.

9. Integration processes are still largely underestimated and undervalued for their contribution to the success of an M&A process, despite sizable research indicating success often pivots on the integration process. Without appropriate considerations for the integration process, organizations will continue to be plagued with many of the issues discussed throughout this research. Organizations must invest the time and resources needed to more effectively manage integration processes for their own operational considerations and for the good of the employees that work for their companies. Failure to progress in this area will continue to impact businesses' bottom lines.

10. Not engaging in proactive strategies generally indicated the organization was engaging in unproductive behaviors. Many of the effective strategies were perceived as ineffective when they were not properly utilized. Companies must stop treating integration processes as transactional tasks, and instead engage with the same levels of intentionality they displayed during the due diligence process to avoid an abundance of unintentional, ineffective behaviors and the problems that result as a consequence of this oversight.

Implications for Action

The results of this research yielded the following implications for action:

1. Despite an increase in the use of M&As to grow businesses, there is still limited information on how to successfully manage an integration process and reduce uncertainty. Additional academic and applied research is needed to build on the body of knowledge about M&As with specific emphasis given to the integration process.

2. Intentional and carefully constructed, timed, and managed communication should be prioritized during every stage of the integration process. During the due diligence process, it is important for employees to hear pertinent information directly from their employer instead of through industry or internal rumor mills. As the integration process continues, employees need ongoing communication to reduce uncertainty. Resources should be invested to develop, employ, and proactively manage a communication plan that seeks to reduce uncertainty, has regular assessments and course corrections built in, and anticipates the needs of the employees.

3. Communication plans should include a variety of organizational channels for communication flow to explain what is happening during the integration process. Firms should consider the use of roadshows, town halls, emails, conference calls, newsletters, websites, and social media.

4. Organizations must create carefully timed opportunities for teams from both organizations to collaborate and work with one another during the integration process. Ideally some of these interactions would be face-to-face. This investment requires the allocation of time and resources, but is critical for reducing uncertainty as the integration process unfolds. Acquiring companies should have an intentional engagement plan to ensure employees in similar roles have ample opportunities to work together and acquired employees have ample opportunities to demonstrate their worth to the new company. This engagement allows the two teams to come together to work toward common goals to improve the organization.

5. An acquiring company should perform a systematic assessment of existing systems, tools, and practices and develop a structured and well-communicated decision-making process to guide integration across organizations. Employees were open to learning new systems and tools when they improved effectiveness or efficiency. Though the acquiring company may be most comfortable integrating new team members into their existing processes, if their systems and tools were outdated, productivity, morale, and uncertainty were impacted. Organizations should consider using pending changes as an opportunity to upgrade systems when appropriate. When new systems and tools are adopted, organizations need to ensure employees are properly trained with ample support.

6. Careful consideration must be given to cultural integration. Finding ways to include components of both cultures in the merging organization reduces uncertainty. Although completely adopting a new culture may not be feasible, a few approaches can be taken. The first approach is to incorporate some aspects of both cultures, essentially building a new culture while keeping some aspects from both communities intact. The second approach is to hold conversations about the cultures and why certain elements may need to be phased out or removed. These conversations can be critical to help when a culture is being dismantled. A third option is to incorporate certain elements of both cultures and slowly remove less critical aspects after the organizations are consolidated.

7. If executives, middle managers, and employees engage in candid dialogue, many integration issues could be resolved or minimized. Employees, middle manager, and executives make assumptions in the absence of having all the facts available, which can increase uncertainty. These miscommunications can result in larger conflicts if the channels for candid communication are not established and if communication is not effectively managed.

8. Organizations engaging in an M&A integration process should document and centralize information to improve future operations and build models of best practices. These models may be specific to each organization, but would allow both organizations to manage and reduce uncertainty while maximizing opportunities for success, minimizing potential risks, and producing information that may be applicable across multiple organizations. The goal of this information would be to establish a better understanding of the integration process to improve the chances for organizations to realize their M&A goals.

9. Organizations should monitor the mental health and wellness of employees and middle managers to manage stress, anxiety, and motivation. Building more robust processes to achieve integration goals could provide organizations with methods to manage these critical aspects. When left unattended, these items can increase uncertainty and hinder employee performance.

10. Middle managers must be provided with a plan, the resources, and the skills needed to achieve success during the integration process. The middle manager role is key within organizations and can help reduce uncertainty as changes occur during integration. With a plan, middle managers can execute the integration process, monitor the mindset of employees, and achieve organizational goals.

11. Natural tension exists between what information should be disclosed to whom and when, and the need to limit information protected by confidentiality agreements. Executives must carefully decide what is important to communicate and what should not be shared. In situations when information cannot be communicated due to confidentiality clauses or when information is withheld because a decision was not finalized, why information cannot be disclosed should be transparently shared. Concerns about confidentiality clauses are valid, but the amount of information shared should be enough to allow employees to function in their daily roles. To reduce uncertainty related to information sharing, executives need to strike a balance. A strategic communication plan can provide relief in this area.

Recommendations for Future Research

Based on the findings and limitations of this study, the recommendations for future studies emerged.

1. Replicate this study with changes to the terminology used for uncertainty, instead changing job-related to individual, structural to team, and strategic to organizational.

2. Replicate this study with a more homogeneous sample of industries to determine if trends are unique to a specific industry.

3. Conduct a similar phenomenological study with an expanded population size based on the same selection criteria to determine the reliability of the data.

4. Conduct a similar phenomenological study, adjusting the interview process to allow for more aggressive follow-up questions that dig deeper into the data.

5. Replicate this study with executives to determine their perceptions of effective and ineffective ways to manage uncertainty during integration.

6. Replicate this study with frontline employees to determine their perceptions of effective and ineffective ways to manage uncertainty during integration.

7. Conduct a similar phenomenological study with homogeneous domain experts (e.g., accounting, human resources, legal experts) to document key tasks in each area that need to be addressed during an integration process.

8. Conduct a qualitative study that examines job-related, structural, or strategic uncertainty individually, thus allowing the researcher to dig deeper into a specific type of uncertainty and recommended strategies.

Concluding Remarks and Reflections

This study investigated how job-related, structural, and strategic uncertainty impacted the M&A integration process from the perspective of middle managers. Many organizations utilized M&As as a means of achieving growth or expanding into new markets, but the research indicated navigating an integration process continues to be challenging. With failure rates ranging from 40-80%, it is apparent this study only grazed the surface of information available for this massive change phenomenon. This study illuminated the need for additional research into both the mechanics of uncertainty within an organization and the integration process for M&As. Many strategies recommended by middle managers are basic change management strategies underutilized throughout the integration process. Furthermore, a model or guiding doctrine would be immensely powerful for an organization undergoing an M&A integration process because they could be working to mitigate possible issues that may be otherwise overlooked. This study provides actionable steps that could help to reduce the failure rate of integrations, limit job-related, structural, and strategic uncertainty during integration, and help organizations maintain or improve the value of M&As.

This researcher found a large disconnect between the overall M&A goals and the efforts put into the integration process. This is alarming given the magnitude of the investments made in M&As. Although companies appeared adept at conducting due diligence into the transactional elements of the organizations for an M&A, they failed to consider the human element until after the deal was completed. The current approach opens organizations to unnecessary risks and potential loss of value due to a lack of forethought and consideration for the integration process.

Managers and executives must be equipped with proper training, skills, and resources needed to successfully manage integration processes. The resources and efforts needed to more effectively manage integration processes are within reach. The cost for using these strategies is a fraction of those associated with a failed M&A deal. The comparison of putting in the time, effort, and resources to achieving a successful integration compared to the potential loss in value because of a poorly conducted integration process should be seriously pondered by companies.

REFERENCES

Able, R. M. (2007). *The importance of leadership and culture to M&A success*. Retrieved from https://imaa-institute.org/docs/m&a/towersperrin_09_the%20 importance_of_leadership_and_culture_to_m-and-a_success.pdf

Ahmad, A., Zia-ur-Rehman, M., & Rashid, M. (2011). Assessing the characteristics of work-related stress in public sector organizations. *Interdisciplinary Journal of Contemporary Research in Business, 2*(10), 511-523.

Allan, S., & Cianni, M. (2011, May). *Middle managers: Their critical - and growing - role in M&A transactions.* Retrieved from https://www.towerswatson.com/en-us/insights/news-letters/global/strategy-at-work/2011/middle-managers-their-critical-and-growing-role-in-m-and-a-transactions

Allatta, J. T., & Singh, H. (2011). Evolving communication patterns in response to an acquisition event. *Strategic Management Journal, 32*(10), 1099-1118. doi:10.1002/smj.930

Alexandris, G., Petmezas, D., & Travlos, N. G. (2010). Gains from mergers and acquisitions around the world: New evidence. *Financial Management, 39*(4), 1671-1695.

Anderson, D. L. (2012). *Organization development: The process of leading organizational change* (2nd ed.). Thousand Oaks, CA: SAGE Publications.

Anderson-Ackerman, L., & Anderson, D. (2010). *The change leader's roadmap: How to navigate your organization's transformation* (2nd ed.). San Francisco, CA: Pfeiffer.

Aon Hewitt. (2011). *Trends in global employee engagement.* Retrieved from http://www.aon.com/attachments/thought-leadership/trends_global_employee_engagement_final.pdf

Appelbaum, S. H., Gandell, J., Shapiro, B. T., Belisle, P., & Hoeven, E. (2000). Anatomy of a merger: Behavior of organizational factors and processes throughout the pre-during-post-stages (part 2). *Management Decision, 38*(10),

674-684.

Appelbaum, S. H., Lefrancois, F., Tonna, R., Shapiro, B. T. (2007) Mergers 101 (part two): Training managers for culture, stress, and change challenges. *Industrial and Commercial Training, 39*(4), 191-200.

Appelbaum, S. H., Roberts, J., & Shapiro, B. T. (2009). Cultural strategies in M&A's: Investigating ten case studies. *Journal of Executive Education, 8*(1), 33-58.

Appelo, J. (2010, October). *Complexity versus lean: The big showdown.* Retrieved from www.slideshare.net/jurgenappelo/complexity-versus-lean

Arendt, L. A., Priem, R. L., & Ndofor, H. A. (2005). A CEO-adviser model of strategic decision making. *Journal of Management, 31*(5), 680-699.

Armstrong, G. (2011). *Leadership in times of change: An examination of a merger experience* (Doctoral thesis). Available from ProQuest Dissertations & Theses. (UMI No. 923876070)

Arons, P. A. (2010). *Middle management communication and interaction practices and their influence on employee satisfaction and motivation* (Doctoral dissertation). Available from ProQuest Dissertations and Theses Database. (UMI No. 3438404)

Bakar, H. A., Mustaffa, C. S., & Mohamad, B. (2009). LMX quality, supervisory communication and team oriented commitment. *Corporate Communication, 12*(1), 11-33.

Baldwin, P. S. (2012). *A grounded theory of change dynamics: Experiences of employees in acquired organizations* (Doctoral dissertation). Available from ProQuest Dissertations and

Theses Database. (UMI No. 3540819)

Balle, N. (2008). Hearts at stake: A theoretical and practical look at communication in connection with mergers and acquisitions. *Corporate Communications: An International Journal, 13*(1), 56-67.

Bardwick, J. M. (2008). *One foot out the door: How to combat the psychological recession that's alienating employees and hurting American business.* New York, NY: AMACON.

Barki, H., & Pinsonneault, A. (2005). A model of organizational integration, implementation effort, and performance. *Organization Science, 16*(2), 165-179.

Basinger, V. L. (2012). *The impact of mergers on those left behind - Maintaining employee engagement after merger-based restructuring in a financial services firm* (Master's thesis). Available from ProQuest Dissertations and Theses Database. (UMI No. 1531808)

Bean, M. H. (2013). *The impact of changes in leaders' environments on the success of strategic merger and acquisition: A phenomenological study of the experience of US healthcare executives in transition* (Doctoral dissertation). Available from ProQuest Dissertations and Theses Database. (UMI No. 3557590)

Bellou, V. (2006). Psychological contract assessment after a major organizational change: The case of mergers and acquisitions. *Employee Relations, 29*(1), 68-88.

Bercovitz, J., & Feldman, M. (2008). Academic entrepreneurs: Organizational change at an individual level. *Organization Science, 19*(1), 69-89.

Bertoncelj, A., & Kovac, D. (2007). An integrated approach for a higher success rate in mergers and acquisitions. *Proceedings of Rijeka School of Economics, 25*(1), 167-188.

Birks, M., & Mills, J. (2015). *Grounded theory: A practical guide* (2nd ed.). Thousand Oaks, CA: SAGE Publications.

Björkman, I., Stahl, G. K., & Vaara, E. (2007). Cultural differences and capability transfer in cross-border acquisitions: The mediating roles of capability complementarity, absorptive capacity, and social integration. *Journal of International Business Studies, 38*(4), 658-672.

Bordia, P., Hobman, E., Jones, L., Gallois, C., & Callan, V. J. (2004). Uncertainty during organizational change: Types, consequences, and management strategies. *Journal of Business and Psychology, 18*(4), 295-316.

Bos, K. V. D. (2007). Hot cognition and social justice judgments: The combined influence of cognitive and affective factors on the justice judgment process. In D. de Cremer (Ed.), *Advances in the psychology of justice and affect* (pp. 59-82). Greenwich, CT: Information Age Publishing.

Bowditch, J. L., & Buono, A. F. (2004). *A primer on organizational behavior* (6th ed.). Hoboken, NJ: John Wiley & Sons.

Braun, D. (2013). *Successful acquisitions: A proven plan for strategic growth*. New York, NY: AMACOM.

Brockner, J., Wiesenfeld, B. M., & Diekmann, K. A. (2009). Towards a "fairer" conception of process fairness: Why, when and how more may not always be better than less. *The Academy of Management Annals, 3*(1), 183-216.

Burke, W. W. (2013). *Organization change: Theory and practice*. Thousand Oaks, CA: SAGE Publications.

Busch, D. (2011). Cultural theory and conflict management in organizations: How does theory shape our understanding of culture in practice. *International Journal of Cross Cultural Management, 12*(1), 9-24. doi:10.1177/1470595811413106

Cameron, K. S., & Quinn, R. E. (2005). *Diagnosing and changing organizational culture: Based on the competing values framework*. Hoboken, NJ: John Wiley & Sons.

Carola, J. M. (2010). *Perceived frequency of change and burnout among employees of varying position levels and organization types* (Doctoral dissertation). Available from ProQuest Dissertations and Theses Database. (UMI No. 3400884)

Cartwright, S., & Schoenberg, R. (2006). Thirty years of mergers and acquisitions research: Recent advances and future opportunities. *British Journal of Management, 17*(S1), 1-5.

Cheng, G. H. L., & Chan, D. K. S. (2008). Who suffers more from job insecurity? A meta-analytic review. *Applied Psychology, 57*(2), 272-303.

Chickene, S. D. (2013). *Targeted M and A performance: Post-acquisition process and organizational integration* (Doctoral dissertation). Available from ProQuest Dissertations and Theses Database. (UMI No. 3640961)

Cho, B. (2004). *Employees' reactions to a merger and acquisitions: A social identity perspective* (Doctoral dissertation). Available from ProQuest Dissertations and Theses Database. (UMI No. 3113482)

Chu, Y. (2012). *Creating value by combining two weak firms: The role of routine disruption in mergers and acquisitions* (Doctoral dissertation). Available from ProQuest Dissertations and Theses Database. (UMI No. 3643433)

Cicero, L., Pierro, A., & Van Knippenberg, D. (2010). Leadership and uncertainty: How role ambiguity affects the relationship between leader group prototypicality and leadership effectiveness. *British Journal of Management, 21*(2), 411-421.

Claremont McKenna College. (2016). *Southern California M&A activity*. Retrieved from http://financial-economics-institute.org/southern-california-ma-activity/

Clayton, B. C. (2010). Understanding the unpredictable: Beyond traditional research on mergers and acquisitions. *Emergence: Complexity and Organization, 12*(3), 1.

Cocco, J. J. (2014). *Team leaders' influence on the relationship between project uncertainty and project progress* (Doctoral dissertation). Available from ProQuest Dissertations and Theses Database. (UMI No. 3684068)

Colquitt, J. A., Greenberg, J., & Zapata-Phelan, C. P. (2005). What is organizational justice? A historical overview. In J. Greenberg & J. A. Colquitt (eds.), *The handbook of organizational justice* (pp. 3-58). Mahwah, NJ: Erlbaum.

Colquitt, J. A., & Salam, S. C. (2009). Foster trust through ability, benevolence, and integrity. In E. Locke (Ed.), *Handbook of principles of organizational behavior: Indispensable knowledge for evidence-based management* (2nd ed., pp. 389-404). Hoboken, NJ: John Wiley & Sons.

Connell, R. (2010). M and A performance improvement: A nontraditional view. *Journal of Management and Marketing Research, 5*, 1-33.

Cope, J. (2003). Entrepreneurial learning and critical reflection discontinuous events as triggers for 'higher-level' learning. *Management Learning, 34*(4), 429-450.

Cording, M., Christmann, P., & King, D. R. (2008). Reducing causal ambiguity in acquisition integration: Intermediate goals as mediators of integration decisions and acquisition performance. *Academy of Management Journal, 51*(4), 744-767.

Creasy, T., Stull, M., & Peck, S. (2009). Understanding employee-level dynamics within the merger and acquisition process. *Journal of General Management, 35*(2), 21.

Cummings, T. G., & Worley, C. G. (2008). *Organization development and change* (9th ed.). Mason, OH: Cengage Learning.

Daly, J. P., Pouder, R. W., & Kabanoff, B. (2004). The effects of initial differences in firms' espoused values on their post-merger performance. *The Journal of Applied Behavioral Science, 40*(3), 323-343.

Danişman, A. (2010). Good intentions and failed implementations: Understanding culture-based resistance to organizational change. *European Journal of Work and Organizational Psychology, 19*(2), 200-220.

David, F.R. (2009). *Strategic management: Concepts* (12th ed.). Upper Saddle River, NJ: Prentice Hall.

De Alwis, A. P. (2013). *Post merger integration leader and acquisition success: A theoretical model of perceived linkages to success of mergers and acquisitions.* (Doctoral dissertation). Available from ProQuest Dissertations and Theses Database. (UMI No. AAI3572551)

De Cremer, D., Brockner, J., Fishman, A., Van Dijke, M., Van Olffen, W., & Mayer, D. M. (2010). When do procedural fairness and outcome fairness interact to influence employees' work attitudes and behaviors? The moderating effect of uncertainty. *Journal of Applied Psychology, 95*(2), 291-304.

De Cremer, D., & Sedikides, C. (2005). Self-uncertainty and responsiveness to procedural justice. *Journal of Experimental Social Psychology, 41*(2), 157-173.

De Cremer, D., & Sedikides, C. (2008). Reputational implications of procedural fairness for personal and relational self-esteem. *Basic and Applied Social Psychology, 30*(1), 66-75.

De Croon, E. M., Sluiter, J. K., Kuijer, F. P., & Frings-Dresen, M. H. (2005). The effect of office concepts on worker health and performance: A systematic review of the literature. *Ergonomics, 48*(2), 119-134.

De Dreu, C. K., & Gelfand, M. J. (2008). The psychology of conflict and conflict management in organizations. In C. K. De Dreu & M. J. Gelfand (Eds.), *The psychology of conflict and conflict management in organizations* (pp. 3-54). New York, NY: Lawrence Erlbaum Associates.

de Haldevang, B. (2009). A new direction in M&A integration: How companies find solutions to value destruction in people-based activity. *Global Business and Organizational Excellence, 28*(4), 6-28. doi:10.1002/joe.20264

De Hoyos, J. L. (2013). *A phenomenological study of merger stress on the acquired manager* (Doctoral dissertation). Available from ProQuest Dissertations and Theses Database. (UMI No. 3567534)

De Lange, A. H., Taris, T. W., Kompier, M. A., Houtman, I. L., & Bongers, P. M. (2002). Effects of stable and changing demand-control histories on worker health. *Scandinavian Journal of Work, Environment, & Health, 28*(2), 94-108.

Dean, D., & Cianni, M. (2011, November). *The manager's role in*

M&A: Implications for the insurance industry. Retrieved from https://www.towerswatson.com/-/media/Pdf/Insights/Newsletters/Global/Emphasis/2011/1101-MandA-FIN1.pdf%3Fla%3Den+&cd=1&hl=en&ct=clnk&gl=us

Deloitte Development, LLC. (2009). *Cultural issues in mergers and acquisitions.* Retrieved from https://www2.deloitte.com/content/dam/Deloitte/us/Documents/mergers-acqisitions/us-ma-consulting-cultural-issues-in-ma-010710.pdf

Deloitte Development, LLC. (2015). *Integration report 2015: Putting the pieces together.* Retrieved from https://www2.deloitte.com/content/dam/Deloitte/no/Documents/mergers-acquisitions/integration-report-2015.pdf

Deloitte Development, LLC. (2016). *M&A trends report, mid-year 2016: Our annual comprehensive look at the M&A market.* Retrieved from https://www2.deloitte.com/content/dam/Deloitte/us/Documents/mergers-acqisitions/us-deloitte-mergers-acquisitions-report-trends-2016.pdf

DePamphilis, D. M. (2009). *Mergers, acquisitions, and other restructuring activities: An integrated approach to process, tools, cases, and solutions* (4th ed.). Burlington, MA: Academic Press.

DePamphilis, D. M. (2014). *Mergers, acquisitions, and other restructuring activities* (7th ed.). San Diego, CA: Academic Press.

Deutsch, C. & West, A. (2010, May). *A new generation of M&A: A McKinsey perspective on the opportunities and challenges.* Retrieved from http://webcache.googleusercontent.com/ search?q=cache:XpvERK_rFAEJ:www.mckinsey.com/~/media/mckinsey/dotcom/client_service/Organization/PDFs/775084%2520MM%2520new%2520generation%25202%252010.ashx+&cd=1&hl=en&ct=clnk&gl=us

Dickens, P. M. (2012). *Facilitating emergence: Complex, adaptive systems theory and the shape of change* (Doctoral dissertation). Available from ProQuest Dissertations and Theses Database. (UMI No. 3516072)

Dickinson, S. (2013). *Best practices in integrating acquisitions* (Master's thesis). Available from ProQuest Dissertations and Theses Database. (UMI No. 1541784)

DiGeorgio, R. (2002). Making mergers and acquisitions work: What we know and don't know–part II. *Journal of Change Management, 3*(3), 259-274.

Doseck, K. E. (2012). *A phenomenological study of HRM practitioner merger and acquisition integration preparation: Perspectives on organizational culture, human capital management, and change management* (Doctoral dissertation). Available from ProQuest Dissertations and Theses Database. (UMI No. 3498080)

Dunbar, J. K. (2013). *The role of organizational leadership capability in mergers & acquisitions* (Doctoral dissertation). Available from ProQuest Dissertations and Theses Database. (UMI No. 3592867)

El Hag, F. L. (2009). *Impact of organizational culture on success of mergers and acquisitions: An analytical study* (Doctoral dissertation). Available from ProQuest Dissertations and Theses Database. (UMI No. 1468579)

Ellis, R. A. (2013). *Visual communication in organization change:*

The impact of cognitive load on understanding and adoption (Doctoral dissertation). Available from ProQuest Dissertations and Theses Database. (UMI No. 3569813)

Erkama, N. (2010). Power and resistance in a multinational organization: Discursive struggles over organizational restructuring. *Scandinavian Journal of Management, 26*(2), 151-165.

Erwin, D. G., & Garman, A. N. (2010). Resistance to organizational change: Linking research and practice. *Leadership & Organization Development Journal, 31*(1), 39-56.

Fairbank, C. (2006). *Combining organizations: The role of perceived organizational values* (Doctoral dissertation). Available from ProQuest Dissertations and Theses Database. (UMI No. 3247230)

Fedor, D. B., Caldwell, S., & Herold, D. M. (2006). The effects of organizational changes on employee commitment: A multilevel investigation. *Personnel Psychology, 59*(1), 1-29.

Ferry, F. J. (2010). *Transactional and transformational leadership performance: Organizational level, job function, and role affects on ratee outcomes* (Doctoral dissertation). Available from ProQuest Dissertations and Theses Database. (UMI No. 3405142)

Fink, N. (2010). The high cost of low morale: How to address low morale in the workplace through servant leadership. *Leading Edge Journal, 3*(2), 1-10.

Ford, J. D., Ford, L. W., & D'Amelio, A. (2008). Resistance to change: The rest of the story. *Academy of management Review, 33*(2), 362-377.

Funk, M. M. (2011). *The best strategies to lead organizational change during the pre-merger phase* (Doctoral dissertation). Available from ProQuest Dissertations and Theses Database. (UMI No. 1500274)

Furst-Holloway, S., & Cable, D. M. (2008). Employee resistance to organizational change: Managerial influence tactics and leader-member exchange. *Journal of Applied Psychology, 93*(2), 453-462.

Gallego-Toledo, J. M. (2015). *The relationship between perceived frequency of change and the wellbeing of telecom professionals* (Doctoral dissertation). Available from ProQuest Dissertations and Theses Database. (UMI No. 3672416)

Gallup Consulting. (2011, September). *State of the global workplace 2011*. Retrieved from http://www.gallup.com/services/177083/state-global-workplace-2011.aspx

Galpin, T. J., & Herndon, M. (2014). *The complete guide to mergers and acquisitions: Process tools to support M&A integration at every level*. Hoboken, NJ: John Wiley & Sons.

Gara, T. (2013, August). In charts: Why middle managers matter [Blog]. Retrieved from http://blogs.wsj.com/corporate-intelligence/2013/08/06/in-charts-why-middle-managers-matter/

Geiselmann, B. G. (2012). *How individuals whose companies have been acquired transition organizational cultures successfully* (Doctoral dissertation). Available from ProQuest Dissertations and Theses Database. (UMI No. 3512502)

George, G. (2011). *Combining organization development (OD) and organization design: An investigation based on the perspectives of OD and change management consultants* (Doctoral dissertation). Available from ProQuest Dissertations and

Theses Database. (UMI No. 3443321)

Gerds, J., Strottmann, F., & Jayaprakash, P. (2010). *Post merger integration: Hard data, hard truths.* Retrieved from https://dupress.deloitte.com/dup-us-en/deloitte-review/issue-6/post-merger-integration-hard-data-hard-truths.html

Gilley, A., McMillan, H. S., Gilley, J. W. (2009). Organizational change and characteristics of leadership effectiveness. *Journal of Leadership & Organizational Studies, 16*(1), 38-47.

Grover, V., & Malhotra, M. K. (2003). Transaction cost framework in operations and supply chain management research: theory and measurement. *Journal of Operations management, 21*(4), 457-473.

Guindon, K. M. (2013). *An interpretive phenomenological analysis of pharmaceutical industry frontline management during post-acquisition integration* (Doctoral dissertation). Available from ProQuest Dissertations and Theses Database. (UMI No. 3576347)

Gupta, B., & Sharma, N. K. (2008). Compliance with bases of power and subordinates' perception of superiors: Moderating effect of quality of interaction. *Singapore Management Review, 30*(1), 1.

Hahm, S. D., Jung, K., & Moon, M. J. (2013). Shaping public corporation leadership in a turbulent environment. *Public Administration Review, 73*(1), 178-187.

Harding, D., & Rouse, T. (2007, April). *Human due diligence.* Retrieved from https://hbr.org/2007/04/human-due-diligence

Hart, A. J. S. M. A., & Sherman, A. (2006). *Mergers & acquisitions from A to Z* (2nd ed.). New York, NY: AMACON.

Herd, T. J., & McManuse, R. (2012). *Who says M&A doesn't create value?* Retrieved from https://www.scribd.com/document/79856227/Accenture-Outlook-Who-Says-M-A-Doesn-t-Create-Value

Hogg, M. A. (2007). Uncertainty–identity theory. *Advances in Experimental Social Psychology, 39,* 69-126.

Hopkins, H. D. (2008). Cross-border mergers and acquisitions: do strategy or post-merger integration matter? *International Management Review, 4*(1), 5.

Institute for Mergers, Acquisitions & Alliances. (2018a). *M&A statistics.* Retrieved from https://imaa-institute.org/mergers-and-acquisitions-statistics/

Institute for Mergers, Acquisitions & Alliances. (2018b). *United States - M&A statistics.* Retrieved from https://imaa-institute.org/m-and-a-us-united-states/

Ihidero, S. O. (2011). *Examining the relationships between organizational communication and conflict management, and the leader member exchange (LMX) theory* (Doctoral dissertation). Available from ProQuest Dissertations and Theses Database. (UMI No. 3509191)

Isern, J., & Pung, C. (2007). *Driving radical change.* Retrieved from http://www.mckinsey.com/business-functions/organization/our-insights/driving-radical-change

Ishii, K. (2006). The effects of social information through communication networks on attitudes about organizational change. In *Conference Papers--International Communication Association* (pp. 1-31).

Jacobs, G., van Witteloostujin, A., & Christe-Zeyse, J. (2013). A theoretical framework of organizational change. *Journal of Organizational Change Management, 26*(5), 772-792.

Jansson, N. (2013). Organizational change as practice: A critical analysis. *Journal of Organizational Change Management, 26*(6), 1003-1019.

Jarrard, D. (2014). What to say, when to say it. *Trustee, 67*(3), 30-32.

Jian, G. (2011). Articulating circumstance, identity and practice: Toward a discursive framework of organizational changing. *Organization, 18*(1), 45-64.

Jones, E., Watson, B., Gardner, J., & Gallois, C. (2004). Organizational communication: Challenges for the new century. *Journal of Communication, 54*(4), 722-750.

Kale, P., & Singh, H. (2009). Managing strategic alliances: What do we know now, and where do we go from here. *Academy of Management Perspectives, 23*(3), 45-62.

Kansal, S., & Chandani, A. (2014). Effective management of change during merger and acquisition. *Procedia Economics and Finance, 11*, 208-217.

Kavanagh, M. H., & Ashkanasy, N. M. (2006). The impact of leadership and change management strategy on organizational culture and individual acceptance of change during a merger. *British Journal of Management, 17*(S1), 81-103.

Khan, S. I. (2013). *Workplace incivility in relation to employees' job strains: The function of role ambiguity, intentional ambiguity, and employees' attribution* (Doctoral dissertation). Available from ProQuest Dissertations and Theses Database. (UMI No. 3556931)

Kiefer, T. (2005). Feeling bad: Antecedents and consequences of negative emotions in ongoing change. *Journal of Organizational Behavior, 26*(8), 875-897.

Kim, S., & Roumeliotis, G. (2014, June). *Global mergers and acquisitions are at a seven-year high.* Retrieved from http://www.businessinsider.com/r-global-ma-at-seven-year-high-as-big-corporate-deals-return-2014-30

King, D. R., Dalton, D. R., Daily, C. M., & Covin, J. G. (2004). Meta-analyses of post-acquisition performance: Indications of unidentified moderators. *Strategic Management Journal, 25*(2), 187-200.

Knilans, G. (2009). Mergers and acquisitions: Best practices from successful integration. *Employment Relations Today, 35*(4), 39-46. doi:10.1002/ert.20224

Kohut, A. M. (2010). *Significant workplace change: Perspectives of survivors* (Doctoral dissertation). Available from ProQuest Dissertations and Theses Database. (UMI No. 3404845)

Kotter, J. P. (2007). Leading change: Why transformation efforts fail. *Harvard Business Review, 85*(1), 96-103.

KPMG, LLP. (2011). *Whitepaper on post merger people integration.* Retrieved from https://www.scribd.com/document/323138713/Post-Merger-People-Integration

KPMG, LLP. (2014). *The boom is back: M&A reemerges as leading growth strategy.* Retrieved from http://www.execed.kpmg.com/content/PDF/kpmg-ma-outlook-2015-web.pdf

Krug, J. A. (2009). Brain drain: Why top management bolts after M&As. *Journal of Business Strategy, 30*(6), 128-141.

Kulp, L. E. (2012). *Supervision factors that predict trainee role con-*

flict and role ambiguity (Doctoral dissertation). Available from ProQuest Dissertations and Theses Database. (UMI No. 3542668)

Lakshman, C. (2011). Postacquisition cultural integration in mergers & acquisitions: A knowledge-based approach. *Human Resource Management, 50*(5), 605-623. doi:10.1002/hrm.20447

Larbi-Apau, J. A., & Moseley, J. L. (2009). Communication in performance-based training and instruction: From design to practice. *Performance Improvement, 48*(9), 7-16.

Lehman, C. M., & DuFrene, D. D. (2011). *Business communication*. Retrieved from http://www.cengage.com/resource_uploads/downloads/0324782179_248744.pdf

Leroy, H., Palanski, M. E., & Simons, T. (2012). Authentic leadership and behavioral integrity as drivers of follower commitment and performance. *Journal of Business Ethics, 107*(3), 255-264.

Levay, C. (2010). Charismatic leadership in resistance to change. *The Leadership Quarterly, 21*(1), 127-143.

Liang, X., Ndofor, H. A., Priem, R. L., & Picken, J. C. (2010). Top management team communication networks, environmental uncertainty, and organizational performance: A contingency view. *Journal of Managerial Issues, 22*(4), 436-455.

Lincoln, Y. S., & Guba, E. G. (1985). *Naturalistic inquiry*. Beverly Hills, CA: SAGE Publications.

Lind, E. A., & Van den Bos, K. (2002). When fairness works: Toward a general theory of uncertainty management. *Research in Organizational Behavior, 24*, 181-223.

Lodorfos, G., & Boateng, A. (2006). The role of culture in the merger and acquisition process: Evidence from the European chemical industry. *Management Decision, 44*(10), 1405-1421.

Lombard, M., Snyder-Duch, J., & Bracken, C. C. (2004). *Practical resources for assessing and reporting inter-coder reliability in content analysis research projects.* Retrieved from http://www.temple.edu/sct/mmc/reliability/

Loorbach, D., & Rotmans, J. (2010). The practice of transition management: Examples and lessons from four distinct cases. *Futures, 42*(3), 237-246.

Maepa, T. P. (2014). *Success and failure factors in post-acquisition/post-merger integration* (Doctoral thesis). Available from ProQuest Dissertations & Theses. (UMI No. 1703998479)

Mahajan, N. (2011). *Uncertain times call for certain measures: Assessing domains and means of uncertainty reduction* (Doctoral dissertation). Available from ProQuest Dissertations and Theses Database. (UMI No. 3466371)

Malik, T., & Kabiraj, S. (2010). Intra-Organizational Interpersonal Communication and Uncertainty Reduction in a Technology Firm. *International Journal of Business Insights & Transformation, 4*(1), 46-56.

Mann, A. (2011). *Managing uncertainty during organization design decision-making processes: The moderating effects of different types of uncertainty* (Doctoral dissertation). Available from ProQuest Dissertations and Theses Database. (UMI No. 3453258)

Mao, Y. (2010). *Does culture matter? Relating intercultural communication sensitivity to conflict management styles, technology use, and organizational communication satisfaction* in *multinationals in China* (Doctoral dissertation). Available from ProQuest Dissertations and Theses Database. (UMI No. 3423497)

Marks, M. L., & Mirvis, P. H. (2011). Merge ahead: A research agenda to increase merger and acquisition success. *Journal of Business and Psychology, 26*(2), 161-168.

Maurer, R. (2003). Why chance works. *The Journal for Quality and Participation, 26*(4), 38.

McMillan, J. H., & Schumacher, S. (2010). *Research in education: Evidence-based inquiry* (7th ed.). Upper Saddle River, NJ: Pearson Higher Education.

Miranda, R., Fontes, M., & Marroquin, B. (2008). Cognitive content-specificity in future expectancies: Role of hopelessness and intolerance of uncertainty in depression and GAD symptoms. *Behaviour Research and Therapy, 46*(10), 1151-1159.

Money, R. K., Jr. (2011). *Transformational leadership as a success factor in a merger* (Doctoral dissertation). Available from ProQuest Dissertations and Theses Database. (UMI No. 3460874)

Morgan, D., & Zeffane, R. (2003). Employee involvement, organizational change and trust in management. *International Journal of Human Resource Management, 14*(1), 55-75.

Muller, N. J. (2006). Mergers and managers: What's needed for both to work? Reflections on a merger of two higher education libraries in KwaZulu-Natal. *South African Journal of Libraries and Information Science, 72*(3), 198-207.

Nguyen, H., & Kleiner, B. H. (2003). The effective management of mergers. *Leadership & Organization Development Journal,*

24(8), 447-454.

Nikandrou, I., Papalexandris, N., & Bourantas, D. (2000). Gaining employee trust after acquisition: Implications for managerial action. *Employee Relations, 22*(4), 334-355.

Nikolaou, I., Vakola, M., & Bourantas, D. (2011). The role of silence on employees' attitudes "the day after" a merger. *Personnel Review, 40*(6), 723-741.

Nesterkin, D. A. (2013). Organizational change and psychological reactance. *Journal of Organizational Change Management, 26*(3), 573-594.

Ooghe, H., Van Laere, E. De Langhe, T. (2006). Are acquisitions worthwhile? An empirical study of the post-acquisition performance of privately held Belgian companies. *Small Business Economics*, Volume 27(2), 223-243.

Oreg, S. (2006). Personality, context, and resistance to organizational change. *European Journal of Work and Organizational Psychology, 15*(1), 73-101.

Oreg, S., & Berson, Y. (2011). Leadership and employees' reactions to change: The role of leader's personal attributes and transformational leadership style. *Personal Psychology, 63*(3) 627-659. doi:10.1111/j.1744-6570.2011.01221.x

Osterman, P. (2008). *The truth about middle managers: Who they are, how they work, why they matter.* Boston, MA: Harvard Business Press.

Outlay, C. N. (2008). *Resizing the IS function after outsourcing: Examining psychological contracts, violations and outcomes* (Doctoral dissertation). Available from ProQuest Dissertations and Theses Database. (UMI No. 3327430)

Papadakis, V. (2007). Growth through mergers and acquisitions: How it won't be a loser's game. *Business Strategy Series, 8*(1), 43-50.

Paruchuri, S., Nerker, A., & Hambrick, D. C. (2006). Acquisition integration and productivity losses in the technical core: Disruption of inventors in acquired companies. *Organization Science, 17*(5), 545-562.

Patten, M. L. (2012). *Understanding research methods: An overview of the essentials* (8th ed.). Glendale, CA: Pyrczak Publishing.

Patton, M. Q. (2002). *Qualitative research & evaluation methods* (3rd ed.). Thousand Oaks, CA: SAGE Publications.

Peloquin, J. (2011). *An investigative case study of human capital in mergers and acquisitions* (Doctoral dissertation). Available from ProQuest Dissertations and Theses Database. (UMI No. 3443646)

PricewaterhouseCoopers, LLP. (2011). *People integration: Capturing M&A value by making the most of human capital post deal.* Retrieved from http://www.pwc.com/us/en/deals/mergers-acquisitions/assets/pwc-people-integration.pdf

PricewaterhouseCoopers, LLP. (2014). *M&A integration: Looking beyond the here and now.* Retrieved from http://www.pwc.com/us/en/deals/publications/assets/pwc_ma_integration_survey_report_2014.pdf

Puranam, P., Singh, H., & Zollo, M. (2006). Organizing for innovation: Managing the coordination-autonomy dilemma in technology acquisitions. *Academy of Management Journal, 49*(2), 263-280.

Pyc, L. S. (2011). *The moderating effects of workplace ambiguity* and perceived job control on the relations between abusive supervision and employees' behavioral, psychological, and physical strains* (Doctoral dissertation). Available from ProQuest Dissertations and Theses Database. (UMI No. 3454834)

Quach, H. (2013). *An analysis of organizational trust and communication effectiveness* (Doctoral dissertation). Available from ProQuest Dissertations and Theses Database. (UMI No. 3557876)

Quinones-Gonzalez, L. E. (2013). *A psychological contract perspective of employees' reactions to organizational change: An assessment of the impact of mergers and acquisitions on survivors within pharmaceuticals in Puerto Rico* (Doctoral thesis). Available from ProQuest Dissertations & Theses. (UMI No. 1666808015)

Ragatz, G. L., Handfield, R. B., & Petersen, K. J. (2002). Benefits associated with supplier integration into new product development under conditions of technology uncertainty. *Journal of Business Research, 55*(5), 389-400.

Rahim, M. A. (2001). *Managing conflict in organizations.* Westport, CT: Quorum Books.

Ralston, P. (2014). *Supply chain collaboration: A literature review and empirical analysis to investigate uncertainty and collaborative benefits in regards to their practical impact on collaboration and performance* (Doctoral dissertation). Available from ProQuest Dissertations and Theses Database. (UMI No. 3627448)

Reider, M. C. (2011). *The role of leadership traits in driving organizational life cycle decisions* (Doctoral dissertation). Available from ProQuest Dissertations and Theses Database.

(UMI No. 3590592)

Roberson, J. (2004). *An analysis of email as a communications tool in the organizational workplace environment* (Doctoral dissertation). Available from ProQuest Dissertations and Theses Database. (UMI No. 3132467)

Robinson, W. T. (2011). *Organizational complexity and leadership*. Retrieved from http://www.antiochne.edu/wp-content/uploads/2012/08/RobinsonLeadershipPaperFall2011.pdf

Roh, B. E. (2011). *Organizational structural factors leading to financially successful mergers and acquisitions: A phenomenological case study* (Doctoral dissertation). Available from ProQuest Dissertations and Theses Database. (UMI No. 3452421)

Romano, S. D. (2014). *Leading at the edge of uncertainty: An exploration of the effect of contemplative practice on organizational leaders* (Doctoral dissertation). Available from ProQuest Dissertations and Theses Database. (UMI No. 3672785)

Sanders, K., and Frenkel, S. (2011). HR-line management relations: characteristics and effects. *The International Journal of Human Resource Management, 22*(8), 1611-1617.

Saunders, M. N. K., Altinay, L., & Riordan, K. (2009). The management of post-merger cultural integration: implications from the hotel industry. *Services Industries Journal, 29*(10), 1359-1375.

Schmidt, J., (2008). *Making mergers work – the strategic importance of people*. Alexandria, VA: Society for Human Resource.

Schweiger, D. M., & Very, P. (2003). Creating value through

merger and acquisition integration. In S. Finkelstein & C. Cooper (eds.), *Advances in mergers and acquisitions* (pp. 1-26). Bingley, United Kingdom: Emerald Group Publishing Limited.

Sengupta, D., & Ramadoss, S. (2011). *Employee engagement: Unlocking the secrets to nurturing a productive workforce.* New Delhi, India: Bizantra.

Seo, M. G., & Hill, N. S. (2005). Understanding the human side of merger and acquisition: An integrative framework. *The Journal of Applied Behavioral Science, 41*(4), 422-443.

Shen, L. (2016, June). *These are the 12 biggest mergers and acquisitions of 2016.* Retrieved from http://fortune.com/2016/06/13/12-biggest-mergers-and-acquisitions-of-2016/

Sher, R. (2012, March). *Why half of all M&A deals fail, and what you can do about it.* Retrieved from http://www.forbes.com/sites/forbesleadership-forum/2012/03/19/why-half-of-all-ma-deals-fail-and-what-you-can-do-about-it/#48cef37f20ae

Shermon, G. (2011). *Post merger people integration: Forward.* Retrieved from https://www.scribd.com/document/323138713/Post-Merger-People-Integration

Shook, C. L., Priem, R. L., & McGee, J. E. (2003). Venture creation and the enterprising individual: A review and synthesis. *Journal of Management, 29*(3), 379-399.

Skalik, J., Barabasz, A., & Belz, G. (2002). Polish managers and the change management process: A management learning perspective. *Human Resource Development International, 5,*

377-382.

Smith, M. E. (2002). Implementing organizational change: Correlates of success and failure. *Performance Improvement Quarterly, 15*(1), 67-83.

Smollan, R. K., & Sayers, J. G. (2009). Organizational culture, change and emotions: A qualitative study. *Journal of Change Management, 9*(4), 435-457.

Stahl, G. K., & Voigt, A. (2008). Do cultural differences matter in mergers and acquisitions? A tentative model and examination. *Organization Science, 19*(1), 160-176.

Steele, D. M. (2014). *Mergers & Acquisitions: The roles of cultural/relational fit and human integration in cultural/relational convergence and organizational commitment* (Doctoral dissertation). Available from ProQuest Dissertations and Theses Database. (UMI No. 3586274)

Steelman, C. M. (2009). *Corporate leadership and the working environment: Relationships among organizational leadership factors in a corporate post-merger working environment* (Doctoral dissertation). Available from ProQuest Dissertations and Theses Database. (UMI No. 3372588)

Stensaker, I. G., & Langley, A. (2009). Change management choices and trajectories in a multidivisional firm. *British Journal of Management, 21*(1), 7-27.

Stillman, T. F., & Baumeister, R. F. (2009). Uncertainty, belongingness, and four needs for meaning. *Psychological Inquiry, 20*(4), 249-251.

Stoker, J. I. (2006). Leading middle management: Consequences of organizational changes for tasks and behaviors of middle managers. *Journal of General Management, 32*(1),

31-42.

Strange, J. M., & Mumford, M. D. (2002). The origins of vision: Charismatic versus ideological leadership. *Leadership Quarterly, 13*(4), 343-377.

Sun, K. (2011). *Inter-unit conflict, conflict resolution methods, and post-merger organizational integration in healthcare organizations* (Doctoral dissertation). Available from ProQuest Dissertations and Theses Database. (UMI No. 3482282)

Swaminathan, V., Murshed, F., & Hulland, J. (2008). Value creation following merger and acquisition announcements: The role of strategic emphasis alignment. *Journal of Marketing Research, 45*(1), 33-47.

Szabla, D. B. (2007). A multidimensional view of resistance to organizational change: Exploring cognitive, emotional, and intentional responses to planned change across perceived change leadership strategies. *Human Resource Development Quarterly, 18*(4), 525-558.

Tannous, G. F., & Cheng, B. (2007). Canadian takeover announcements and the job security of top managers. *Canadian Journal of Administrative Sciences, 24*(4), 250.

Taylor, S. J., Bogdan, R., & DeVault, M. (2015). *Introduction to qualitative research methods: A guidebook and resource.* Hoboken, NJ: John Wiley & Sons.

Thau, S., Aquino, K., & Wittek, R. (2007). An extension of uncertainty management theory to the self: the relationship between justice, social comparison orientation, and antisocial work behaviors. *Journal of Applied Psychology, 92*(1), 250.

Thau, S., Bennett, R. J., Mitchell, M. S., & Marrs, M. B. (2009). How management style moderates the relationship between abusive supervision and workplace deviance: An uncertainty management theory perspective. *Organizational Behavior and Human Decision Processes, 108*(1), 79-92.

Thayser, D. (2014). Chapter 13: Mergers and acquisitions. In J. Fouche (Ed.), *Financial management - Turning theory into practice* (pp. 566-613). Cape Town, South Africa: Oxford University Press.

Thomas, R., Sargent, L. D., & Hardy, C. (2011). Managing organizational change: Negotiating meaning and power-resistance relations. *Organization Science, 22*(1), 22-41.

Tikhomirov, A., A, & Spangler, W. D. (2009). Neo-charismatic leadership and the fate of mergers and acquisitions: An institutional model of CEO leadership. *Journal of Leadership & Organizational Studies, 17*(1), 44-60. doi:10.1177/1548051809351537

Towers Perrin. (2003). *Working today: Understanding what drives employee engagement.* Retrieved from http://www.keepem.com/doc_files/Towers_Perrin_Talent_2003(TheFinal).pdf

Towers Perrin. (2005). *Reconnecting with employees: Quantifying the value of engaging your workforce.* Retrieved from http://www.lombard-media.lu/pdf/0509_TP_Engagement.pdf

Ullrich, J., Wieseke, J., & Dick, R. V. (2005). Continuity and change in mergers and acquisitions: A social identity case study of a German industrial merger. *Journal of Management Studies, 42*(8), 1549-1569.

U.S. Department of Labor. (2016a). *Labor force statistics from the current population survey.* Retrieved from https://www.bls.gov/cps/demographics.htm#age

U.S. Department of Labor. (2016b). *Data retrieval: Employment, hours, and earnings (CES).* Retrieved from https://www.bls.gov/webapps/legacy/cesbtab1.htm

Valant, L. B. (2009). Why do both marriages and business mergers have a 60% failure rate. *CPA Journal, 81*(9), 15-22.

Van den Bos, K., & Lind, E. A. (2002). Uncertainty management by means of fairness judgments. *Advances in Experimental Social Psychology, 34*, 1-60.

Van den Bos, K. (2009). Making sense of life: The existential self trying to deal with personal uncertainty. *Psychological Inquiry, 20*(4), 197-217.

Vander Elst, T., Baillien, E., De Cuyper, N., & De Witte, H. (2010). The role of organizational communication and participation in reducing job insecurity and its negative association with work-related well-being. *Economic and Industrial Democracy, 31*(2), 249-264. doi:10.1177/0143831X09358372

Vasconcelos, F. C., & Ramirez, R. (2011). Complexity in business environments. *Journal of Business Research, 64*(3), 236-241.

Vasilaki, A. (2011). The relationship between transformational leadership and postacquisition performance. *International Studies of Management & Organization, 41*(3), 42-58.

Vazirani, N., & Mohapatra, S. (2012). Merging organizational culture through communication - 'post mergers & acquisitions'. *SIES Journal of Management, 8*(1), 31.

Venema, W. H. (2015). Integration: The critical M&A success factor. *Journal of Corporate Accounting and Finance, 26*(4), 23-27. doi:10.1002/jcaf.22046

Vollmer, C. (2016, January). *2016 state of the U.S. labor force.* Retrieved from https://jobenomicsblog.com/2016-state-of-the-u-s-labor-force/

Wagner, R., & Harter, J. K. (2006). *12: The great elements of managing.* Washington, DC: The Gallup Organization.

Waldman, D., & Javidan, M. (2009). Alternative forms of charismatic leadership in the integration of mergers and acquisitions. *The Leadership Quarterly, 20*(2) 130-142.

Wallis, C., Steptoe, S., & Cole, W. (2006). Help! I've lost my focus. *Time Magazine, 167*(2), 47-53.

Weber, Y. & Drori, I. (2011). Integrating organizational and human behavior perspectives on mergers and acquisitions: Looking inside the black box. *International Studies of Management & Organization, 41*(3), 76-95.

Weber, Y., Rachman-Moore, D., & Tarba, S. Y. (2012). HR practices during post-merger conflict and merger performance. *International Journal of Cross Cultural Management, 12*(1), 73-99.

Weber, Y., Tarba, S., & Oberg, C. (2014). *A comprehensive guide to mergers & acquisitions: Managing the critical success factors across every stage of the M&A process.* Upper Saddle River, NJ: FT Press.

Weber, Y., Tarba, S. Y., & Reichel, A. (2011). A model of the influence of culture on integration approaches and international mergers and acquisitions performance. *International Studies of Management & Organization, 41*(3), 9-24.

Weiner, S., & Hill, R. (2008). Seven steps to merger excellence. *Ivey Business Journal Online, 72*(5).

Retrieved from http://iveybusinessjournal.com/publication/seven-steps-to-merger-excellence/

Whitaker, S. C. (2012). *Mergers & acquisitions integration handbook: Helping companies realize the value of acquisitions.* Hoboken, NJ: John Wiley & Sons.

Yukl, Gary A. (2006). *Leadership in organizations* (6th ed.). Saddle River, NJ: Prentice Hall.

Zoller, H. M., & Fairhurst, G. (2007). Resistance leadership: The overlooked potential in critical organization and leadership studies. *Human Relations, 60*(9), 1331-1360.

Zollo, M., & Meier, D. (2008). What is M&A performance? *The Academy of Management Perspectives, 22*(3), 55-77.

Zollo, M., & Singh, H. (2004). Deliberate learning in corporate acquisitions: post-acquisition strategies and integration capability in US bank mergers. *Strategic Management Journal, 25*(13), 1233-1256.

APPENDICES

APPENDIX A:

Interview Script

Introduction

My name is Joe Pazmany and I am currently completing my Doctorate in Organizational Leadership through Brandman University. A colleague of mine, [referral name], suggested you would be an excellent candidate for this research. The title of the study is Merger and Acquisition Integration: Exploring Uncertainty from the Perspective of the Middle Manager. This study is looking into how middle managers perceive uncertainty during the integration process. The goal will be to use these findings to generate new information for practitioners and organizations to use to their benefit.

Purpose Statement

The purpose of this qualitative study was to explore middle managers' perceptions about how organizations managed job-related, structural and strategic uncertainty during a merger and acquisition integration process. Furthermore, this research investigated what strategies middle managers perceived effective and ineffective for managing job-related, structural and strategic uncertainty during a merger and acquisition integration process. Finally, this study worked to identify the strategies middle managers recommended to manage job-related, structural and strategic uncertainty during a merger or acquisition integration process.

Focus of the Study

This study will explore three distinct types of uncertainty based of previous uncertainty models. Job-related uncertainty pays attention to how uncertainty plagues employees at an individual level. Structural uncertainty looks at the impacts of uncertainty on day-to-day operations. Strategic uncertainty focuses on the uncertainty regarding rationale for the change, the organization's direction, and the shifting environment of the organization.

Disclaimer

I will be conducting a 12-question interview that will probe job-related, structural, and strategic uncertainty and your experience with it during integration. All interviews will be recorded and saved on a password protected computer.

All participation in this research is voluntary. You can withdraw from the interview and study at any point in time without any repercussions. If you have any questions or concerns regarding the research or study, please feel free to contact Joe Pazmany or the study's dissertation chair.

Participant Background

Could you give me some insight into your background as a manager over the last few years?

Interview Questions

Job-Related Uncertainty

1. Based on your lived experience, how did your organization manage job-related uncertainty during a merger and acquisition integration process?
2. Based on your lived experience, what specific strategies did your organization use that were perceived to be effective for managing job-related uncertainty during a merger and acquisition integration process?
3. Based on your lived experience, what specific strategies

did your organization use that were you perceived to be ineffective for managing job-related uncertainty during a merger and acquisition integration process?
4. What specific strategies would you recommend to manage job-related uncertainty during a merger and acquisition integration process?

Structural Uncertainty
1. Based on your lived experience, how did your organization manage structural uncertainty during a merger and acquisition integration process?
2. Based on your lived experience, what specific strategies did your organization use that were perceived to be effective for managing structural uncertainty during a merger and acquisition integration process?
3. Based on your lived experience, what specific strategies did your organization use that were you perceived to be ineffective for managing structural uncertainty during a merger and acquisition integration process?
4. What specific strategies would you recommend to manage structural uncertainty during a merger and acquisition integration process?

Strategic Uncertainty
1. Based on your lived experience, how did your organization manage strategic uncertainty during a merger and acquisition integration process?
2. Based on your lived experience, what specific strategies did your organization use that were perceived to be effective for managing strategic uncertainty during a merger and acquisition integration process?
3. Based on your lived experience, what specific strategies did your organization use that were you perceived to be ineffective for managing strategic uncertainty during a merger and acquisition integration process?
4. What specific strategies would you recommend to manage strategic uncertainty during a merger and acquisition integration process?

Probing Questions
1. Can you elaborate and go into more detail?
2. Do you have a story or illustration that would help me understand that?

Conclusion

Thank you for your time. At this point we have concluded the interview session. After I finish gathering data, I will be publishing my findings and will be sending you a complete copy of my results. Thank you again.

APPENDIX B:

Invitation Email

Dear Participant,

I hope my email finds you in good spirits. My name is Joe Pazmany and I am currently completing my Doctorate in Organizational Leadership through Brandman University. A colleague of mine, [referral name], suggested you would be an excellent candidate for a research study I am putting together.

The title of the study is Merger and Acquisition Integration: Exploring Uncertainty from the Perspective of the Middle Manager. This study is looking into how middle managers perceive uncertainty during the integration process. The goal will be to use these findings to generate new information for practitioners and organizations to use to their benefit.

I am requesting 45 minutes to conduct a 12-question interview. Depending upon your availability this can either be in person or through a virtual meeting place such as Skype. The interview questions will focus on job-related, structural, and strategic uncertainty and your experience with these types of uncertainty during an integration process. The definitions for these types of uncertainty are as follows:

Job-Related Uncertainty – Pays attention to how uncertainty plagues employees at an individual level.

Structural Uncertainty – Looks at the impacts of uncertainty on day-to-day operations.

Strategic Uncertainty – Focused on the uncertainty regarding rationale for the change, the organization's direction, and the shifting environment of the organization.

    I invite you to join me to create new knowledge that can enhance current and future managers. Upon the conclusion of this study, all the findings will be summarized and sent back to you. If you are interested in being a participant in this study, please respond to this email or contact me.

Your consideration is truly appreciated.

Respectfully,

Joe Pazmany

APPENDIX C:

Informed Consent

Information About: Merger and Acquisition Integration - Exploring Uncertainty from the Perspective of the Middle Manager

Brandman University
16355 Laguna Canyon Road
Irvine, CA 92618

Responsible Investigator: Joe Pazmany

Purpose of the Study

The purpose of this qualitative study was to explore middle managers' perceptions about how organizations managed job-related, structural and strategic uncertainty during a merger and acquisition integration process. Furthermore, this research investigated what strategies middle managers perceived effective and ineffective for managing job-related, structural and strategic uncertainty during a merger and acquisition integration process. Finally, this study worked to identify the strategies middle managers recommended to manage job-related, structural and strategic uncertainty during a merger or acquisition integration process.

This study is being performed for the purposes of research only.

If you agree to the study, you will be invited to participate in a 45-minute interview that can be done in person or through Skype depending upon your availability. The interview will have twelve questions focusing on the three types of uncertainty and how they impact your organization amidst integration and your experience. You may choose to not answer a question if you are not comfortable and you can stop your participation in the interview at any time.

The interview will be recorded to ensure accuracy of your responses. These recorded interviews will be put on a secure hard drive until the interviews can be transcribed. Upon completion of all the transcripts, all recordings will be permanently deleted. The computer that will house these documents will be password protected. All personal information such as your real name will be coded to protect your privacy and all participants will be given a numeric value to ensure confidentiality. No personal information will be used past the initial interview to ensure that all participant privacy is secure.

Your experience and knowledge will enhance to the body of literature that currently exists. At the conclusion of the research, all findings will be compiled and available to for your use after the study is over.

All participation in this research is voluntary. You can withdraw from the interview and study at any point in time without any repercussions. Even if you sign this document, you will still be able to change your mind or stop participating in the study at any time. If the study changes in any way, you will be directly notified and must agree to the new terms of the research before continuing to participate. If you have any questions or concerns regarding the research or study, please feel free to contact Joe Pazmany or the study's dissertation chair.

Please make sure to read carefully through this Informed Consent document, the Participant Bill of Rights, and to ask the researcher any questions you may have before agreeing to participate in this study.

By signing this document, you are providing your consent to participate in the Merger and Acquisition Integration: Exploring Uncertainty from the Perspective of the Middle Manager study.

You may contact the researcher at any point in the process if you have questions or issues with any part of the study or the research.

I agree to participate in this study.

_____

I agree to have my interview voice recorded as part of this study.

_____

Research Participant's Bill of Rights

Any person who is requested to consent to participate as a subject in an experiment, or who is requested to consent on behalf of another, has the following rights:

1. To be told what the study is attempting to discover.
2. To be told what will happen in the study and whether any of the procedures, drugs or devices are different from what would be used in standard practice.
3. To be told about the risks, side effects or discomforts of the things that may happen to him/her.
4. To be told if he/she can expect any benefit from participating and, if so, what the benefits might be.
5. To be told what other choices he/she has and how they may be better or worse than being in the study.
6. To be allowed to ask any questions concerning the study both before agreeing to be involved and during the study.
7. To be told what sort of medical treatment is available if any complications arise.
8. To refuse to participate at all before or after the study is started without any adverse effects.
9. To receive a copy of the signed and dated consent form.
10. To be free of pressures when considering whether he/she wishes to agree to be in the study.

If at any time you have questions regarding a research study, you should ask the researchers to answer them. You also may contact the Brandman University Institutional Review Board, which is concerned with the protection of volunteers in research projects.

The Brandman University Institutional Review Board may be contacted either by telephoning the Office of Academic Affairs at (949) 341-9937 or by writing to the Vice Chancellor of Academic Affairs, Brandman University, 16355 Laguna Canyon Road, Irvine, CA, 92618.

www.ingramcontent.com/pod-product-compliance
Lightning Source LLC
LaVergne TN
LVHW011912080426
835508LV00007BA/484